THE IQ

ARGUMENT

THE IQ ARGUMENT

Race, Intelligence and Education

by
H. J. Eysenck

THE LIBRARY PRESS
NEW YORK
1971

Library of Congress Catalog Card Number
71-169974

International Standard Book Number
0-912050-16-0

Printed in U.S.A.

ACKNOWLEDGMENTS

The author gratefully acknowledges permission to quote the following copyrighted material in this book:

A. R. Jensen, *Bulletin of the Atomic Scientist*, Vol. 26, 1970.

A. R. Jensen, *Harvard Educational Review*, Vol. 39, 1969.

P. E. Vernon, *Intelligence and Cultural Environment*, Methuen.

I. I. Gottesman, in *Social Class, Race and Psychological Development*, Holt, Rinehart & Winston.

A. M. Shuey, *The Testing of Negro Intelligence,* Social Science Press.

M. M. de Lemos, "Development of Conservation in Aboriginal Children," *International Journal of Psychology*, No. 4, 1969.

J. Wren-Lewis, "Science and Social Responsibility," *New Society*, No. 426, Vol. 16, 1970.

J. Mercer, "Issues and Dilemmas in School Desegregation, a Case Study," 17th Annual Western Regional Conference on Testing Problems; Copyright ©1968 by Educational Testing Service.

For the figures: (1) W. A. Kennedy, V. Van De Riet and J. C. White, *Monographs of the Society for Research in Child Development*, 28, Ser. No. 90, 1963; (2) T. Dobzhansky, *Mankind Evolving*, Yale University Press; (3) and (4) W. S. Pollitzer, *American Journal of Physical Anthropology*, No. 16, 1958; (5b) L.M. Terman and M. A. Merrill, *Measuring Intelligence*, Houghton Mifflin; (6) H. J. Eysenck, *Know Your Own IQ* and *Check Your Own IQ*, Pelican Books; (7a)

John Ertl; (7b) John Ertl, *Nature*, Vol. 26, 1970; (8) and (9) C. E. Noble, *Perspectives in Biology and Medicine*, Vol. 13, No. 1, 1963; (11), (12), and (13) A. R. Jensen; (14) and (15) A. R. Jensen, "Environment, Heredity and Intelligence," *Harvard Educational Review*, 1969.

For the tables: (1) A. R. Jensen, "Environment, Heredity and Intelligence," *Harvard Educational Review*, 1969; (2) and (3) Sir Cyril Burt; (4) and (5) J. Mercer, "Issues and Dilemmas in School Desegregation: a Case Study," 17th Annual Western Regional Conference on Testing Problems, Copyright © 1968 by Educational Testing Service.

TABLE OF CONTENTS

PREFACE

THE CONTROVERSY about IQ testing, the inheritance of intelligence, and the alleged inferiority of Negroes on IQ tests was fanned into white heat by the publication in the *Harvard Educational Review* of Dr. Arthur Jensen's monograph on "How much can we boost IQ and scholastic achievement?" Sunday supplements like the *New York Times Magazine*, and picture journals like *Life* took the matter up,* and shock waves from this explosion are still being felt. Annually Dr. William Shockley, the Nobel Laureate and inventor of the transistor, appeals to the National Academy of Sciences to undertake scientific research into problems of racial differences in intelligence, and annually his request is turned down—a clear case of the abdication of scientific responsibility. Nor is the debate confined to the U.S.A. In England, too, research is revealing considerable scholastic backwardness and low IQ scores among colored children, and considerable argument was started by Jensen's visit to London and Cambridge last year, and by the views he voiced at various public meetings. Clearly, the problems raised are not likely to go away quietly. They have to be faced, and discussed on a

*Lee Edson, "Jensenism," *New York Times Sunday Magazine*, August 31, 1969; John Neary, "Jensenism: Variations on a Racial Theme," June 12, 1970: *Life Magazine*.

rational basis. This book aims to present the relevant facts, with as little interpretation as possible; only knowledge of these facts makes it possible to come to any sort of rational conclusion.

I approached writing this book with much hesitation, and not a little aversion. Having always been out on the radical wing in my political opinions, and having taken it as axiomatic that there could not be any genetically determined differences between races, it caused me much emotional stress to delve into the scientific literature which seemed to suggest very strongly that I might be wrong. This accounts for my aversion. I also wondered if it was wise at this juncture to write on a topic which was so explosive, and to say things which might add to the trials and tribulations of a group of people who had already suffered so much, and were continuing to suffer, at the hands of white men. This accounts for my hesitation. I also knew, of course, that whatever conclusion I might come to, readers with closed minds would not only refuse to look at the evidence, or trust in the facts, but would blame me personally for a state of affairs for which ultimately Nature (rather than I) must be held responsible. Nothing I can say will alter this inevitable hostility.

There are two points I wish to make here, although I have made them again in more detail in the main body of the book. They are so important that repetition may serve to underline their relevance to the discussion. The first point is that whatever conclusion we may come to with respect to the hereditary contribution to the Negro's low IQ, as compared with the white American's, *this conclusion does not, and cannot, justify any argument in favor of segregation. Segregation on racial grounds is morally wrong and ethically unacceptable.* No conceivable facts could persuade me that segregation should become the law of the land. It is important to get this point out of the way, because to many people the argument about hereditary determination of IQ, and of racial differences, seems closely bound up with a social policy of segregation. There is no such bond. Racists would still favor segregation, even though Negroes could be shown to be genetically and in every other way equal to whites; their feelings are not dependent on factual research, or on details of IQ differences. We must keep apart our search for facts, and our decisions on social policy of segregation or desegregation; the latter are moral judgments, the former are not. Jensen, to give but one example, testified in Washington in favor of desegregation, in spite of his stated belief that the evidence supported a genetic interpretation of part, at least, of the Negro inferiority on IQ tests. Clearly, he appreciated the lack of connection between fact and morality better than some of his critics.

The second point is that factual research is important, for the simple reason that good will is not enough in helping the black man climb out of his disadvantaged status, and become the equal of the white man. Many efforts have been made during the inter-war period to improve the status of the Negro, and undoubted advances have been made in education, in employment, and in other directions. Yet between the wars the percentage of Negro draftees scoring above the white average on the Armed Forces Qualification Test fell from 13 percent to 7 percent. This increase in the differentiation between the groups does not suggest that what was being done to help the black man was necessarily the right sort of thing, and the failure of "Headstart" and other educational ventures has caused many people convinced of our moral duty to do everything in our power to help him pull himself up to a higher level, to doubt the efficacy of the methods currently in vogue. Only scientific knowledge can tell us just what the problem is, and how to set about solving it; good will is needed, but it does not suffice by itself. If our attempts to help are based on false premises, then our efforts will do more harm than good. Hence the desperate need for research—and hence one's despair at the blindness of the National Academy of Sciences in refusing to see that what is sauce for the physical sciences is sauce for the social sciences as well.

If the reader does not like some of the facts that emerge, I hope against hope that he will not blame me for their existence. I, too, do not like many of the facts, but as a scientist I cannot feel that my duty, in all conscience, is other than to tell what I know. Human life is full of tragedy, defined in the Greek sense as the opposition of two rights. The opposition of the moral belief in the equality of men to the scientific fact of hereditary inequality may be the source of such tragedy. I believe that research can help us overcome this opposition, but not by throwing away either our moral principles, or our scientific integrity. There are obvious difficulties in retaining both, but I think we must make the effort; and only time will tell whether such an effort can in the long run be successful.

H.J. EYSENCK

Institute of Psychiatry,
Maudsley Hospital,
London

INTRODUCTION

MORE YEARS AGO than I care to remember, I was boxing for my College when one evening our coach came to me and said that I was fighting a Negro. "Watch it," he said "these niggers have heads made of iron. Never punch him on the chin. Go for the midriff." "Oh, yes!" I thought, "there goes Mr. Racial Prejudice. I've heard of these stereotypes; you'd be a fool to believe in that sort of nonsense." . . . However, I said nothing, and went into my fight without paying much heed to the warning. Nothing happened in the first round, but in the second my opponent dropped his guard for a second, and I hit him on the chin with one of the best blows I ever managed. (I was never very good at boxing, and gave it up soon afterwards.) He hardly blinked an eye, but my hand seemed to explode. For a moment I thought I had broken a bone. It felt rather like one of those cartoon films where you can see the hand visibly swelling and getting bright red. For the rest of the fight (which ended in a draw) I never hit another blow with my right.

Here you have, in miniature form, two attitudes which confront each other over more serious matters than boxing: on the one hand, the presumed knowledge that two races differ innately with respect to some physical or mental trait, and on the other the presumed knowledge that this belief is all prejudice, and that there are no such differences. Both are equally unscientific, in the absence of clear-cut evidence, but both are apt to be very firmly held. I still do not know whether the coach was in fact right, or whether I was just unlucky; this too is not an uncommon conclusion to come to. We know very little, and if the reader expects any definite answer to the questions raised in the title and sub-title of this book, he will almost certainly be disappointed. Most people who write on this topic seem to know all the answers, and are firmly convinced that their point of view is correct. I know perfectly well that we do not know all the answers, and feel little confidence that such views as I have formed are necessarily correct. What I have tried to do in this book has been to discuss such evidence as exists, and to draw such conclusions from it as are reasonable at this point. If these conclusions fall short of certainty, and do not satisfy the reader, then he should blame the lack of adequate research in this field. I can only draw attention to what has been done, and warn against over-interpreting data that admit of different ways of looking at their implications. However, even this may be a service that some may find useful; it is not likely to appeal to those who feel they already know the truth, and do not need scientific experiments to support (or discredit?) their firmly held views.

Such a book, discussing in a popular and nontechnical vein rather complex experimental designs and empirical tests, would not be worth writing were it not for the tremendous importance of the issues raised. It is no exaggeration to say that among the problems which face humankind, that of race is one of the most difficult, recalcitrant, and ominous. If we cannot solve it sooner rather than later, it threatens to engulf us in strife, both civil and international, which will make previous wars and commotions seem trivial.

The problems associated with race are difficult enough when viewed calmly and from the scientific point of view; they become completely impossible of solution when emotion is allowed to enter. The problem discussed in this book is only one of those associated with race, yet there is no doubt that political and social beliefs and emotions have become strongly tied up with it. South Africans and white citizens of the southern states of the U.S.A. will not tolerate any views contradicting their firmly held beliefs in the innate inferiority of Negroes. "Don't confuse us with facts," they say, "our minds are made up." Conversely, most middle-class Europeans, and the so-called intelligentsia in the northern states of the U.S.A., are equally certain that such alleged differences do not exist; they, too, often show little desire to investigate scientifically the evidence for what they feel in their bones to be the truth. Name-calling frequently ensues when the battle-lines are so crudely drawn. "Racists" and "nigger-lovers" are two frequently-used epithets thrown by one side against the other. This book will please neither side, as it concludes that neither position is adequately backed by scientifically ascertained facts. It will probably infuriate "racists" by also concluding that even if there were a genetic element in the inferiority of certain groups (not "races"; some white groups are inferior to other white groups, and some colored groups are superior, others inferior, to white groups) this would have no bearing on the question of segregation. But it is hoped that the book may please the large number of intelligent people who are genuinely puzzled by the opposing war-cries of entrenched "experts" who declare in favor of what seem to be entirely contradictory conclusions. It is also hoped that it may cool down the heat developed in the course of this struggle, and even develop some light by which to read the future development of the argument, however dimly.

IS IT POSSIBLE to adopt the neutrality required by science in a field which generates so much emotion? There is empirical evidence that "racialist" attitudes on purely psychological issues relating to the inheritance of intelligence and innate differences between races are more frequently found among conservative psychologists, while "nigger-loving" attitudes are more frequently found among liberal and socialist psychologists. Whether the political belief causes the scientific position to be held, or whether the scientific conclusions drawn determine the political belief, is immaterial. There seems to be some tendency for the two to go together, and the reader is consequently entitled to ask in which direction the writer's own political and social beliefs and attitudes go. This is an unusual position, but the logic of the facts suggest that such a "declaration of interest," as it is called in Parliament, is not out of place.

My recognition of the importance of the racial problem, and my own attitudes of opposition to any kind of racial segregation, and hatred for those who suppress any sector of the community on grounds of race (or sex, or religion) were determined in part by the fact that I grew up in Germany, at a time when Hitlerism was becoming the very widely held doctrine which finally prevailed and led to the death of several million Jews whose only crime was that they belonged to an imaginary "race" which had been dreamed up by a group of men in whom insanity was mixed in equal parts with craftiness, paranoia with guile, and villainy with sadism. No one who ever heard Hitler in full spate, as I did when all of us Berlin school children were herded into the Tempelhofer Feld to listen to one of his tirades, is ever likely to underrate the strength of the emotions involved in racial hatred. My own reaction was one of hatred for these purveyors of hatred, intolerance for these apostles of intolerance, but not unreasoning opposition for these protagonists of unreason. It seemed to me then, as it seems to me now, that human problems, like all other problems, have to be settled on a factual basis. Emotion and prejudice cannot be overcome by contrary emotion and prejudice, but only by careful factual research, unencumbered by bias and determined to follow the evidence wherever it may lead. Facts, of course, are one thing; deducing social policies from these facts is quite another. Such deductions are (and must be) largely determined by social, ethical, and religious beliefs. Even if it were demonstrated that American Negroes were intellectually inferior to American whites for reasons partly under genetic control, it would by no means follow that segregation was justified, or that an inferior system of education was adequate for them. It could just as well be argued that Negroes required, and should be provided with, a better system of education to remedy these defects in so far as that was possible, and that research should be done into how best such remedial teaching could be arranged and organized, and on what principles it could best proceed.

Why, then, bother at all with writing about the facts if social policy is not dictated by them? Why conduct research, if the results of this research are not to lay the foundations of political action? I shall return to these questions at the end of this book. Here I merely want to emphasize the point that facts are one thing, attitudes another. A benevolent attitude towards non-white races, coupled with admiration for their many outstanding qualities, and deep sympathy for their suffering, should not blind one towards such evidence as may exist to indicate that with respect to certain qualities there may be genetic differences favoring one race (or ethnic subgroup) as against another. Such differences as have been suggested in the field of intelligence by empirical research do not by any means always favor the white groups; as we will see, "racialist" interpretations of certain findings would suggest the inferiority of certain white groups. If benevolence is missing, then no evidence for genetic inferiority of intelligence is needed to set up the concentration camps and the gas chambers; Hitler and his henchmen never asserted that Jews were intellectually inferior! A "racist," to me, is one who views other races with hatred, distrust and dislike; one who wishes to subordinate them and keep them in an inferior position. An "egalitarian," to me, is one who feels friendly to all other races, likes their members and feels favorably inclined towards them, one who has no wish to appear in a superior position towards them, or to dominate them in any way. These attitudes are not logically related to a demonstration that different racial groups are, or are not, innately equal with respect to psychological abilities, personality traits, temperamental characteristics, motivational indices, or what not. I am not a racist for believing it possible that Negroes may have special innate gifts for certain athletic events, such as sprints, or for certain musical forms of expression. I am not a racist for taking seriously the empirical demonstration that Maoris are superior on tests of verbal fluency to whites. Nor am I a racist for seriously considering the possibility that the demonstrated inferiority of American Negroes on tests of intelligence may, in part, be due to genetic causes. I would be a racialist if I did not consider very seriously, and without bias, all alternative hypotheses suggested to account for the observed facts, or if I deduced from the facts such conclusions as that segregation was justified. It is important to keep these two issues well separated; facts are one thing, attitudes are another. To deny the importance of this separation is to deny the possibility of serious scientific study of social problems.

IT IS, OF COURSE, POSSIBLE that one's attitudes and beliefs come into conflict with the facts. A well-known example is the case of J.B.S. Haldane, the scientist and Communist, who was faced with this problem when Lysenko's absurd pseudo-scientific claims in genetics and plant biology were taken up by Stalin and the Communist leadership in Russia. As a Communist, his sympathies dragged him to the defence of Lysenko; as a scientist, he knew that Lysenko's claims were untrue. His scientific honesty finally triumphed, and he withdrew from the Communist Party. Similarly, I found it very difficult to look at the evidence detailed in this book with a detached mind, in view of the fact that it contradicted certain egalitarian beliefs I had considered almost axiomatic. Others may share this difficulty, but in the interests of all sides it must be overcome. Lasting and satisfactory solutions to social problems are not likely to be built on factually erroneous premises.

But can we really take what the experts say seriously, when the experts seem to be at loggerheads themselves? There has been so much discussion, often impassioned, in which geneticists oppose geneticists, psychometricians psychometricians, that the layman may be excused for wondering if this is not all bogus material that he is being asked to consider, presented by people who are only venting their spleen. There are a number of reasons why this appealing notion is in fact wrong, and why we can put some faith in what the experts say. In the first place, we must be sure we are referring to "experts," in the true sense (that is, people who have specialized in the relevant fields of behavioral genetics, psychometrics, and intelligence testing, have contributed significantly to these areas, and are familiar with the enormous amount of research which is relevant to a discussion of the field). Just as the term "star" has become degraded from its earlier use which referred to really outstanding actors and musicians, so the term "expert" has become degraded until every hopeful young PhD, and every academic who is roped into a discussion on radio or television, is referred to as an "expert," although he may know very little more about the issue in question than the man in the street. Most of the "experts" who discussed the "Jensenist heresy" which I shall be dealing with in the next chapter were of the second kind; often experts in their own fields, but not particularly knowledgeable in the field under discussion.

It is important to realize just what this implies. Even a hundred years ago, there were "universalists" who could claim to be knowledgeable in many different sciences; this is no longer possible. Even within a single science, specialization has become the rule, and in psychology, say, an expert in psychometrics will not know very much about learning theory, or recent work on emotion, or perception, or psychophysics, or any of at least a dozen other disciplines within psychology. This is recognized in most sciences, and an expert on rheology would not expect to discuss recent work on cosmology, nor would an expert in cryogenics talk about gas chromatography. Psychologists are less modest. They are often impelled by their *daimon* to talk on subjects which may interest them, but in which they are not expert. (Psychiatrists are even worse, but let that pass.) When you read in the papers that "experts" have disagreed, it is always wise to find out first whether they were in fact expert in the subject under discussion. Confusions of this kind have spread the impression that, on the subject this book deals with, there is really very little agreement. Nothing could be farther from the truth. There is far more agreement than disagreement, and I shall return to this point again later on.

Even when experts agree, however, they can often give the impression that they do not, and the techniques for achieving this result are worthy of more detailed study than they have so far received. Let me mention a few ploys which I have noted in looking through the many discussions which have taken place on the subject of this book. I have given them names so that they can be more easily recognized. Number one is called the "I like cheese, you like strawberries" ploy. Both statements are true (or may be true), and there is no contradiction between them. Get two highly trained academics on to the subject, however, and in no time they will be able to work up what looks like a genuine disagreement. You may think that this trick should be too obvious to work, but substitute technical terms for cheese and strawberries, and sprinkle with some mathematical formulae, and the layman is lost immediately. Number two ploy is called the "this tumbler is half full—no, it's half empty" one. Again, in its simple form it is obvious enough, but let academics have a go at it and you will see the fur fly. Number three is the "squirrel on the tree" ploy; this is a little more complex. Suppose you stand in front of a tree, with a squirrel on the side opposite. You now go round the tree, and so does the squirrel, always keeping the tree between you two, until you get back to your starting point. Have you gone round the squirrel, or have you not? This is good for hours of merry disagreement, unless you define exactly what you mean by "going round"—either looking first at the face of the squirrel, then at the side, then at the back, and then at the other side, finishing up with the face (in this sense you haven't gone round the animal) or being first north of the animal, then west, then south, then east, and finally north again (in this sense you have).

These are some of the more popular entertainments; there are many others. Denying what has not been asserted; asserting what has not been denied; arguing about what you think should or would follow from your opponent's position (but which he doesn't think should or would follow); introducing irrelevant points which establish that you are a good guy and he is a bad guy (like being in favor of mother love)—one could write a book on these techniques. What I am trying to establish is simply that it is easy to make it appear that there is disagreement when in reality there is very considerable agreement. The layman cannot readily see through this kind of smoke-screen and may give up in disgust, saying with feeling that "experts always disagree." This is just not so. It is simply that the vast areas on which there is universal agreement are not "news" and are not likely to come to the attention of the man in the street. I would be prepared to assert that experts (real experts, that is) would agree with at least 90% of what I am going to say—probably the true figure would be a good deal higher, but there is no point in exaggerating. Even where they might disagree, the points would be the less crucial ones, and the disagreement would be about shades of emphasis rather than about fundamental issues. I have tried to indicate where I am giving my own opinion, so that readers can form their own views on the points in question. For the rest, I am simply an interpreter of the factual evidence as it appears to me, and as I know it appears to the majority of those working in this field.

ONE LAST WORD about documentation. This is not meant to be a scientific monograph, with complete citation of references; if it were, there would be no room for the rest. The two books to which reference will be made most often—Arthur Jensen's *Environment, Heredity, and Intelligence* and A.M. Shuey's *The Testing of Negro Intelligence*, contain over forty pages of references between them (with very little over-lap); readers who wish to look at the original material on which my presentation is based must get their references from the few books I have quoted at the end of this volume. Let them be reassured that I have consulted not only these books, but above all the primary references therein given. On a few occasions I have mentioned individual references in the text, because these are not mentioned in the books themselves. But for the most part the reader will have to rely on the general watchfulness of my colleagues to make sure that I have not tried to slip anything over on him.

In preparing this book for publication I was very much aided by Professor A.R. Jensen, who communicated to me many detailed findings from his ongoing research, as yet unpublished, and discussed various controversial points with me. I am also indebted to Professor R. Heber, who allowed me to refer to his uniquely interesting but hitherto unpublished work on the possibilities of training intelligence in disadvantaged Negro children, and who also discussed his work with me. Thanks are due to Professor I.I. Gottesman, for permission to quote from his work, and for taking part in an "At Home" with Jensen and other experts at which various problems in this general area were discussed. I am also indebted to Professor A.J. Gregor, who arranged a conference on "Human Differences and Social Issues" at the Maudsley Hospital in London (August 1970), at which many of the leading experts from various countries expressed their views. I benefited much from participating, and learned a great deal about ongoing work not likely to be published for several years.

1
THE JENSENIST HERESY

IN 1653 Pope Innocent X condemned the heresy of Jansenism, proposed by Cornelius Jansen, Bishop of Ypres, as espousing doctrines of "total depravity, irresistible grace, lack of free will, predestination and limited atonement." More recently, social scientists, educationalists and others have condemned a novel heresy, called "Jensenism" by the *New York Times*, after Arthur Jensen, Professor of Educational Psychology at the University of California, Berkeley, and author of a widely discussed review of methods of boosting intelligence which appeared in the *Harvard Educational Review* in 1969. For stressing the importance of inherited factors in the determination of individual differences in human intelligence, he too was declared guilty of believing in "lack of free will and predestination."

Jensen's work certainly drew attention to some problems which previously used to be swept under the mat. Among these problems was that of the genetic determination of racial differences in intelligence. While only constituting a minute part of his article (less than 5%) his assertions—or more correctly, what were supposed to be his assertions—were widely reported (or more correctly, misreported) in the press and on the other mass media. Thus he was supposed to have asserted that scientific evidence proved Negroes to be innately inferior to whites in intelligence; that Negroes should receive a different type of education from whites; and (by inference) that segregation was an appropriate method of dealing with the racial problem in education. If this were indeed the "Jensenist heresy," then the widespread criticism which it has attracted, both in the U.S.A. and abroad, would be not only understandable but salutary. As it happens, his paper does not suggest any of these things, either directly or by inference. In fact, Jensen has testified against segregation before the Washington committee, and has written: "I have always advocated dealing with persons as individuals, each in terms of his own merits and characteristics and I am opposed to according treatment to persons solely on the basis of their race, color, national origin or social class background."

Why then all the fuss? Perhaps the answer lies in the continuation of the above quotation, in which Jensen says: "But I am also opposed to ignoring or refusing to investigate the causes of the well-established differences among racial groups in the distribution of educationally relevant traits, particularly IQ." By refusing to be deterred from including among the hypotheses to be investigated genetic as well as environmentalistic ones, Jensen stepped on many toes in an academic world which for many years had been used to considering only environmentalistic factors, from nutrition to family environment, and from number of books available to number of children in the classroom. There are skeletons in the cupboards even of academic communities, and this particular one has been with us for quite some time. A brief discussion of the history of this particular problem may be relevant.

WHEN THE U.S.A. ENTERED the First World War, widespread testing was undertaken of the mental abilities of the enlisted men, and the results of these intelligence tests (used in part for officer selection—with considerable success!) were later analyzed along many different lines. Marked differences were found *(a)* between men from different states, and *(b)* between men classified as white and Negro. The observed inferiority of the Negro soldiers on these tests was then interpreted (quite erroneously) as evidence of racial inferiority having a genetic basis. The data did not permit any conclusions whatsoever, as no attempts were made to rule out experimentally or statistically alternative hypotheses. In fact, the tests used were rather poor "intelligence" tests (in the sense that they depended too much on educational attainment). The reliance placed on knowledge and information was probably justified for the strictly limited purposes these tests were constructed to serve (men who did poorly because of limited education, rather than because of limited intelligence, were equally unlikely to make good officers within the very short period of time allowed for training). But equally it made the tests almost useless for any scientific purpose. Much attention was given to the overall racial differences observed; it was forgotten that whites from some of the southern states (where educational facilities were generally poor) did rather worse than Negroes from some of the northern states (where education was rather better). Thus a myth of innate racial inferiority was born, reared on alleged scientific study through the use of intelligence tests. Needless to say, these data are not considered very seriously nowadays by any properly trained psychologist.

As a reaction against the fallacies of this type of "research," and in support of a more acceptable and humane attitude, there arose another opposed myth. This might be called the myth of "racial equality is a proven scientific fact." It was enshrined in the famous declaration of an expert committee set up by UNESCO which declared, in 1951, that: "According to present knowledge there is no proof that the groups of mankind differ in their innate mental characteristics, whether in respect of intelligence or temperament. The scientific evidence indicates that the range of mental capacities in all ethnic groups is much the same." As P.E.

Vernon, probably the foremost expert in the assessment of intelligence in different races and groups, pointed out in his book on *Intelligence and Cultural Environment:* "What they should have added is—there is also no proof that innate mental differences do not exist."

Along similar lines, the U.S. Office of Education maintained in 1966 that: "It is a demonstrable fact that the talent pool in any one ethnic group is substantially the same as in any other ethnic group." And the U.S. Department of Labor declared officially in 1965 that "Intelligence potential is distributed among Negro infants in the same proportion and pattern as among Icelanders or Chinese, or any other group." The Department makes its meaning quite clear by saying: "There is absolutely no question of any genetic differential." And UNESCO, in 1964 decided that "The peoples of the world today appear to possess equal biological potentialities for attaining any civilizational level. Differences in the achievements of different peoples must be attributed to their cultural history." Note the use of terms like "demonstrable," "absolutely no question," and "must," when the very same people who are putting forward these notions declare in the same breath, when attacking those not sharing their views, that nothing is in fact known about these problems! This myth of racial equality, while more acceptable in principle to any liberal and well-meaning person that its opposite, is still a myth: there is no scientific evidence to support it. Indeed as Jensen has pointed out, the *a priori* probability of such a belief is small: "The fact that different racial groups in this country have widely different geographic origins and have had quite different histories which have subjected them to different selective social and economic pressures makes it highly likely that their gene pools differ for some genetically conditioned behavioral characteristics, including intelligence or abstract reasoning ability. Nearly every anatomical, physiological, and biochemical system investigated shows racial differences. Why should the brain be an exception?"

FOR MANY YEARS most social scientists adopted the view, either that equality of innate ability between races had been proved, or else that such evidence as there was had certainly not disproved it. Gradually, however, evidence began to pile up which could not be disregarded, and which eliminated (or seemed to eliminate) more and more of the environmentalistic hypotheses which had been put forward to explain the observed (and continuing) inferiority of Negro children on intelligence tests. This evidence will be discussed presently: here let me just state that those who were concerned with these issues, and who found the evidence piling up disproving their cherished beliefs, had more and more difficulty in compromising between their duty to teach the facts as they saw them, and their belief in the absence of heritable racial differences. What finally swayed the balance in many cases was the publication of Shuey's book on *The Testing of Negro Intelligence*, which brought together all the evidence in one very convincing volume. Where the individual researches had caused one to doubt the adequacy of the environmentalist theory, the combination of so many avenues of approach, all leading to the same conclusion, caused these doubts to become very much more severe. Curiously enough, Shuey's book was hardly reviewed and discussed by the popular mass media; although it is less technical than Jensen's monograph, it somehow did not capture the public imagination. For professional psychologists, however, it marked a very important point in the development of their thinking. Never again could they assert with honesty that the evidence disproved, or even contra-indicated, genetic determinants in the causation of racial differences.

Jensen's monograph, often cited as planting the banner of "racial discrimination" in this field, had in fact very little in it that concerned itself with race at all. His purpose in writing the book was quite different. As so much has been written about it, and as so few people have read (still less understood) what he had to say, it may be useful to allow him to summarize his work in his own words. This is what he has to say, in an article published in March 1970, in the *Bulletin of the Atomic Scientists:*

"First, I reviewed some of the evidence and the conclusions of a nationwide survey and evaluation of the large, federally-funded compensatory education programs made by the U.S. Commission on Civil Rights, which concluded that these special programs had produced no significant improvement in the measured intelligence or scholastic performance of the disadvantaged children whose educational achievements these programs were specifically intended to improve. The massive evidence presented by the Civil Rights Commission suggests to me that merely applying more of the same approach to compensatory education on a still larger scale is not at all likely to lead to the desired results, namely increasing the benefits of public education to the disadvantaged. The well-documented fruitlessness of these well-intentioned compensatory programs indicates the importance of now questioning the assumptions, theories and practices on which they were based.

These assumptions, theories and practices—espoused over the past decade by the majority of educators, social and behavioral scientists—are bankrupt. I do not blame the children who fail to benefit from these programs. A large part of the failure, I believe, has resulted from the failure and reluctance of the vast majority of the educational establishment, aided and abetted by social scientists, to take seriously the problems of individual differences in developmental rates, patterns of ability, and learning styles. The prevailing philosophy has been that all children are basically very much alike—they are all 'average children'—in their mental development and capabilities, and that the only causes of the vast differences that show up as they go through school are due to cultural factors and home influences that mold the child even before he enters kindergarten. By providing the culturally disadvantaged with some of the cultural amenities enjoyed by middle class children for a period of a year or two before they enter school, we are told, the large differences in scholastic aptitude would be minimized and the schools could go on thereafter treating all children very much alike and expect nearly all to perform as 'average children' for their grade in school.

It hasn't worked. And educators are now beginning to say: 'Let's really look at individual differences and try to find a variety of instructional methods and differentiated programs that will accommodate these differences.' Whatever their causes may be, it now seems certain that they are not so superficial as to be erased by a few months of 'cultural enrichment,' 'verbal stimulation,' and the like. I have pointed out that some small-scale experimental intervention programs, which gear specific instructional methods to developmental differences, have shown more promise of beneficial results than the large-scale programs based on a philosophy of general cultural enrichment and multiplication of the resources in already existing programs for the 'average child.'

One of the chief obstacles to providing differentiated educational programs for children with different patterns of abilities, aside from the lack of any detailed technical knowledge as to how to go about this most effectively, is the fact that children in different visibly identifiable sub-populations probably will be disproportionately represented in different instructional programs. This highly probable consequence of taking individual differences really seriously is misconstrued by some critics as inequality of opportunity. But actually, one child's opportunity can be another's defeat. To me, equality of opportunity does not mean uniform treatment of all children, but equality of opportunity for a diversity of educational experiences and services. If we fail to take account either of innate or acquired differences in abilities and traits, the ideal of equality of educational opportunity can be interpreted so literally as to be actually harmful, just as it would be harmful for a physician to give all his patients the same medicine.

I know personally of many instances in which children with educational problems were denied the school's special facilities for dealing with such problems (small classes, specialist teachers, tutorial help, diagnostic services, etc.), not because the children did not need this special attention or because the services were not available to the school, but simply because the children were black and no one wanted to single them out as being different or in need of special attention. So instead, white middle-class children with similar educational problems get nearly all the attention and special treatment, and most of them benefit from it. No one objects, because this is not viewed by anyone as 'discrimination.' But some school districts have been dragged into court for trying to provide similar facilities for minority children with educational problems. In these actions the well-intentioned plaintiffs undoubtedly viewed themselves as the 'good guys.' Many children, I fear, by being forced into the educational mold of the 'average child' from Grade 1 on, are soon 'turned off' on school learning and have to pay the consequences in frustration and defeat, both in school and in the world of work for which their schooling has not prepared them.

I do not advocate abandoning efforts to improve the education of the disadvantaged. I urge increased emphasis on these efforts, in the spirit of experimentation, expanding the diversity of approaches and improving the rigor of evaluation in order to boost our chances of discovering the methods that will work best.

My article also dealt with my theory of two broad categories of mental abilities, which I call intelligence (or abstract reasoning ability) and associative learning ability. These types of ability appear to be distributed differently in various social classes and racial groups. While large racial and social class differences are found for intelligence, there are practically negligible differences among these groups in associative learning abilities, such as memory span and serial and paired-associate rote learning.

Research should be directed at delineating still other types of abilities and at discovering how the particular strengths of each individual's pattern of abilities can be most effectively brought to bear on school learning and on the attainment of occupational skills. By pursuing this path, I believe we can discover the means by which the reality of individual differences need not mean educational rewards for some children and utter frustration and defeat for others.

I pointed out that IQ tests evolved to predict scholastic performance in largely European and North American middle class populations around the turn of the century. They evolved to measure those abilities most relevant to the curriculum and type of instruction, which in turn were shaped by the pattern of abilities of the children the schools were then intended to serve.

IQ or abstract reasoning ability is thus a selection of just one portion of the total spectrum of human mental abilities. This aspect of mental abilities measured by IQ tests is important to our society, but it is obviously not the only set of educationally or occupationally relevant abilities. Other mental abilities have not yet been adequately measured; their distributions in various segments of the population have not been adequately determined; and their educational relevance has not been fully explored.

I believe a much broader assessment of the spectrum of abilities and potentials, and the investigation of their utilization for educational achievement, will be an essential aspect of improving the education of children regarded as disadvantaged.

Much of my paper was a review of the methods and evidence that led me to the conclusion that individual differences in intelligence—that is, IQ—are predominantly attributable to genetic differences, with environmental factors contributing a minor portion of the variance among individuals. The heritability of the IQ—that is, the percentage of individual differences variance attributable to genetic factors—comes out at about 80 per cent, the average value obtained from all relevant studies now reported.

These estimates of heritability are based on tests administered to European and North American populations and cannot properly be generalized to other populations. I believe we need similar heritability studies in minority populations if we are to increase our understanding of what our tests measure in these populations and how these abilities can be most effectively used in the educational process.

Although the full range of IQ and other abilities is found among children in every socio-economic stratum in our population, it is well established that IQ differs, on the average, among children from different social class backgrounds. The evidence, some of which I referred to in my article, indicates to me that some of this IQ difference is attributable to environmental differences and some of it is attributable to genetic differences among social classes—largely as a result of differential selection of the parent generations for different patterns of ability.

I have not yet met or read a modern geneticist who disputes this interpretation of the evidence. In the view of geneticist C.O. Carter: 'Sociologists who doubt this show more ingenuity than judgment.' At least three sociologists who are students of this problem—Pitirim Sorokin, Bruce Eckland, and Otis Dudley Duncan—all agree that selective factors in social mobility and assortative mating have resulted in a genetic component in social class intelligence differences. As Eckland points out, this conclusion holds within socially defined class groups but cannot properly be generalized among racial groups, since barriers to upward mobility have undoubtedly been quite different for various racial groups."

JENSEN'S ARGUMENT is thus perfectly general; it is concerned with individual differences and their importance in education. It draws attention to certain facts, such as the failure of "compensatory education" in the U.S.A., and suggests reasons why that failure may have occurred. It advocates attention to certain research findings which suggest new avenues of approach, and which might help to upgrade the educational achievement of less able or academically inclined children. Race only intrudes because of the undisputed fact that Negro children score something like 15 points below white children on intelligence tests, and that these tests have been found empirically (and without depending on any particular theory about what intelligence is) to predict success in school with considerable accuracy.

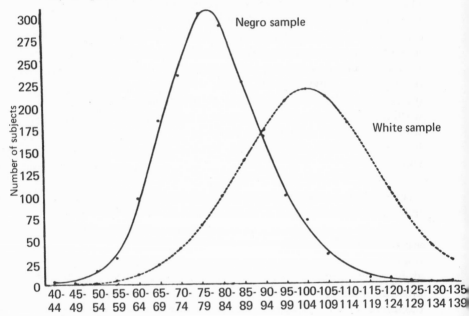

1 Distribution of IQ scores of a sample of Negro and white children, tested in 1960. The graph shows the number of subjects whose scores fall into each five-point interval of IQ (40-44, 45-49 etc.) The mean scores are 80.7 (Negro) and 101.8 (white). The Negro children tested come from the southern states; children from northern states would have shown less marked differences.

The IQ Argument

To illustrate the sort of differences observed, consider Figure 1; this shows the distribution of IQ measures for almost 2,000 randomly selected white children (mean IQ = 101.8) and a sample of almost 2,000 Negro children from southeastern schools (mean IQ = 80.7). This difference of 20 points is typical of Negroes in the south-east; for Negroes in the northern states it would only be half this value (about 10 points) for reasons to be considered presently.

We do not have to make any assumptions about the causes of this discrepancy to see that it must produce considerable difficulties in educational practice, and that when we talk about underprivileged, or educationally retarded children, black children will form a fair proportion of the total sample. It was for this reason that Jensen introduced the "color question," and also added some remarks on the possible importance in it of genetic influences. Much of his monograph deals with the less incendiary, though still much debated, importance of genetic factors in relation to differences in intelligence in white children (for whom alone we have sufficient direct evidence to come to any reasonably well established conclusions.) He presents his reasons for including a discussion of racial differences in the following way:

"The question of race differences in intelligence comes up not when we deal with individuals as individuals, but when certain identifiable groups of subcultures within the society are brought into comparison with one another as groups or populations. It is only when the groups are disproportionately represented in what are commonly perceived as the most desirable and the least desirable social and occupational roles in a society that the question arises concerning average differences among groups. Since much of the current thinking behind civil rights, fair employment, and equality of educational opportunity appeals to the fact there is a disproportionate representation of different racial groups in the various levels of the educational, occupational, and socioeconomic hierarchy, we are forced to examine all the possible reasons for this inequality among racial groups in the attainments and rewards generally valued by all groups within our society. To what extent can such inequalities be attributed to unfairness in society's multiple selection processes? ('Unfair' meaning that selection is influenced by intrinsically irrelevant criteria, such as skin color, racial or national origin, etc.) And to what extent are these inequalities attributable to really relevant selection criteria which apply equally to all individuals but at the same time select disproportionately between some racial groups because there exist, in fact, real average differences among the groups—differences in the population distributions of those characteristics which are indisputably relevant to educational and occupational performance? This is certainly one of the most important questions confronting our nation today. The answer, which can be found only through unfettered research, has enormous consequences for the welfare of all, particularly of minorities whose plight is now in the foreground of public attention. A preordained, doctrinaire stance with regard to this issue hinders the achievement of a scientific understanding of the problem. To rule out of court, so to speak, any reasonable hypotheses on purely ideological grounds is to argue that static ignorance is preferable to increasing our knowledge of reality. I strongly disagree with those who believe in searching for the truth by scientific means only under certain circumstances and eschew this course in favor of ignorance under other circumstances, or who believe that the results of inquiry on some subjects cannot be entrusted to the public but should be kept the guarded possession of a scientific elite. Such attitudes, in my opinion, represent a danger to free inquiry and, consequently, in the long run, work to the disadvantage of society's general welfare. 'No holds barred' is the best formula for scientific inquiry. One does not decree beforehand which phenomena cannot be studied or which question cannot be answered."

MANY CRITICISMS have been expressed and published regarding Jensen's treatment of these issues. The *Harvard Educational Review*, which published the original article, invited seven eminent authorities, critical of Jensen's thesis, to comment in detail. These comments, together with his original paper and a final paper and a final reply, have been bound together and published in book form under the title *Environment, Heredity, and Intelligence*. As he points out in his reply, these critics do not in fact deny any major point of his thesis; they present objections to details, or disagreements about social consequences, but they do not dispute, on the whole, the very scholarly and carefully considered factual part of his thesis. Similarly, most of the numerous critics who have considered his work in various publications have found fault, not so much with what he said, but rather with what they imagined he had said. Such critics often disregarded the numerous qualifications he carefully (and rightly) inserted in order to keep the factual and theoretical record straight. Consider, for example, his main conclusion with respect to Negro-white differences in IQ: ". . . all we are left with are various lines of evidence, no one of which is definitive alone, but which, viewed altogether, make it a not unreasonable hypothesis that genetic factors are strongly implicated in the average Negro-white intelligence difference. The preponderance of evidence is, in my opinion, less consistent with a strictly environmental hypothesis than with a genetic hypothesis, which, of course, does not exclude the influence of environment or its interaction with genetic factors." What he says, clearly, is that the evidence is circumstantial (that is, there is no single, definitive proof for the importance of genetic factors); that the importance of environmental factors, either alone or by interaction with heredity, is not in doubt; but that when all the evidence is considered it does not favor an exclusively environmentalistic hypothesis. I know of no expert in the field of behavioral genetics who would doubt any of these conclusions.

What is meant precisely by this notion that the evidence is circumstantial, and that we must look at many lines of research rather than at any single, decisive experiment? The notion dies hard that scientists put forward a theory, deduce certain consequences, and then perform an experiment which "proves" that theory. This is a complete travesty of the truth. Theories are never proved; if many different deductions are verified, the theory is provisionally accepted as useful, and more and more confidence is put in it as more and more predictions come true. But even the best-established theories (like Newton's theory of gravitation) finally run into difficulties and newer and better theories supplant them. From the beginning of its existence, a new scientific theory encounters facts difficult to bring into its compass. These difficulties—like Mercury's deviant motions in Newton's theory—may never be cleared up, and a new theory altogether may be required to account for them. But until such a new theory is proposed, the old is the best we have (and certainly better than nothing!) Consequently scientists do not put blind confidence in their theories, but regard them as useful and indeed indispensable guides to future advance, and repositories of existing knowledge. The value of a given theory does not rest on any single achievement, however remarkable, nor is its usefulness terminated by any single failure, however serious. Scientists try to keep in mind all the facts, both pro and con, and retain an open mind on the present status of a given theory.

It is along these lines that the theory of genetic involvement in racial differences should be judged. Critics have sometimes haughtily pointed out that this was "only a theory," as if in doing so they contrasted the airy-fairy speculations of Jensen with their own factual, feet-on-the-ground approach. But of course the environmentalist view, too, is a theory, and it too requires support; the question at issue is which way the support is tending. Sociologists often argue as if the environmentalist view was self-evidently true, and required no empirical support. Hence they often fail to look at the evidence against their theories, on the grounds that if what they say is self-evidently right, no evidence can disprove it. Jensen has put forward the counter-argument forcefully, using as his example the observed IQ differences between Indians (American Indians, that is) and Negroes. As he points out, the evidence shows that

"despite greater environmental disadvantage, as assessed by 12 different indices, the Indian children, on the average, exceeded the Negro in IQ and achievement. But I did not pick the environmental indices. The sociologists picked them. They are those environmental factors most often cited by social scientists as the cause of the Negroes' poor performance on IQ tests and in school work. Does not the fact that another group rates even lower than the Negro on these environmental indices (Indians are as far below Negroes as Negroes are below whites), yet displays better intellectual performance, bring into question the major importance attributed to these environmental factors by sociologists? Or should we grant immunity from empirical tests to sociological theories when they are devised to explain racial differences?

There is an understandable reluctance to come to grips scientifically with the problem of race differences in intelligence—to come to grips with it, that is to say, in the same way the scientists would approach the investigation of any other phenomenon. This reluctance is manifested in a variety of 'symptoms' found in most writings and discussions of the psychology of race differences, particularly differences in mental ability. These include a tendency to remain on the remotest fringes of the subject; to sidestep central questions; to blur the issues and tolerate a degree of vagueness in definitions, concepts and inferences that would be unseemly in any other realm of scientific discourse. The writings express an unwarranted degree of skepticism about reasonably well-established quantitative methods and measurements. They deny or belittle already generally accepted facts—accepted, that is, when brought to bear on inferences outside the realm of race differences—and demand practically impossible criteria of certainty before even seriously proposing or investigating genetic hypotheses, as contrasted with extremely uncritical attitudes toward purely environmental hypotheses. There is a failure to distinguish clearly between scientifically answerable aspects of the question and the moral, political, and social policy issues; a tendency to beat dead horses and to set up straw men on what is represented as the genetic side of the argument. We see appeals to the notion that the topic is either really too unimportant to be worthy of scientific curiosity or too complex, or too difficult, or that it is forever impossible for any kind of research to be feasible, or that answers to key questions are fundamentally 'unknowable' in any scientifically acceptable sense. Finally, there is complete denial of intelligence and race as realities, or as quantifiable attributes, or as variables capable of being related to one another and there follows, ostrich-like, dismissal of the subject altogether.

These tendencies will be increasingly overcome the more widely and openly the subject is discussed among scientists and scholars. As some of the taboos against the public discussion of the topic fall away, the issues will become clarified on a rational basis. We will come to know better just what we do and do not yet know about the subject, and we will be in a better position to deal with it objectively and constructively. I believe my article has made a substantial contribution toward this goal. It has provoked serious thought and discussion among leaders in genetics, psychology, sociology and education concerned with these important fundamental issues and their implications for public education. I expect that my work will stimulate further relevant research as well as efforts to apply the knowledge gained thereby to educationally and socially beneficial purposes.

In my view, society will benefit most if scientists and educators treat these problems in the spirit of scientific inquiry rather than as a battlefield upon which one or another preordained ideology may seemingly triumph."

SO MUCH FOR the Jensenist heresy. It will be seen that what he says has been badly distorted in the popular reports. It is clear that most of the criticisms which his work has received are directed, not against his actual words, but against what people thought he had written. And it would seem that we owe him a debt of gratitude for having raised an important problem and for having aroused interest in the further scientific study of these very difficult questions. Whether it was tactful to do so at the time, or in the form it was done, are questions which could be debated endlessly, but which cannot in the nature of things receive a scientific answer. Readers of his monograph can be assured that his review of the evidence relating to the inheritance of individual differences in intelligence is sound, thorough, and as near impartial as it is possible to be.

Where I think he can perhaps be faulted is in his failure to spell out in sufficient detail the consequences which might follow socially from the facts considered. It is only too easy for readers to associate the advocacy of innate sources of intellectual variance between races, which is the position toward which his evidence tends, with an advocacy of segregation and continued suppression of colored people, which has no logical relation to the former point and was certainly far from Jensen's intention. The fact that his position has been interpreted as a racist one may thus in part be his own fault. A psychologist should perhaps be particularly aware of the likely social consequences of his actions. This is particularly true in such a field where emotions are strongly involved, and where the great and grievous injustices which white people have over the centuries done to black people would seem to require more than simple justice now. Some desire for restitution, some acknowledgement of past (and present) guilt, some realization and explicit statement of intent to see that never again would the sins of the whites be visited upon the blacks should perhaps accompany any statements on such matters as the genetic component in racial diversity. It is probably the absence of such evidence of humane and socially responsible considerations in Jensen's book which is in part responsible for the reception it has received.

Certainly most commentators on Jensen's monograph failed to appreciate that Jensen completely shares my own belief (and that of most of his critics) that whatever may be the truth about the inheritance of Negro intelligence, individuals must be judged on the basis of their own personality and accomplishments, not on the basis of their race. Even if we accepted present IQ differences of 15 points or so as definitive, any attempts to classify people into Negroes and whites on the basis of IQ alone would be right only 5% more often than if we decided on the basis of tossing a coin! This is an important point to remember as we go into the complexities of the scientific evidence.

As befits a heretic, Jensen has been accused and tried on many occasions. I, and my colleagues in Britain, will probably best remember the 1970 Cambridge meeting arranged by the British Society for Social Responsibility in Science, at which all the other speakers had been carefully chosen from avowed proponents of the environmentalist doctrine. Their failure to meet his factual arguments did not discourage much of the press from reporting a great victory for environmentalism. Indeed, the position of "Jensenism" on that occasion was not dissimilar to that of the doctrine of "adoptionism" at the Synod of Aachen in 799 AD—and we all know what happened there! Fortunately scientific debates are not settled by newspaper reporters or synods. Let us consider the facts as they emerge from scientific investigations of the issues involved.

2

WHAT IS RACE?

THE VERY TERM, race, has in recent years become an abomination. It has acquired an evil smell combining the stink of the gas ovens in the Nazi concentration camps with the rotting humanity on board the old slave ships America-bound. Yet to recognize facts is not to approve of some of their consequences (or what are imagined to be their consequences—slavery is not always based on race). It was those who are most opposed to the division of society into social classes (the Marxists) who first drew attention to the need to study the importance of class structure in sociological and economic analysis. An interest in the phenomena of race should not be misunderstood as implying approval of the policies, such as *apartheid*, which are sometimes based on race. About the existence of races, after all, there can be little doubt. They are populations that differ genetically and may be distinguishable phenotypically (*i.e.* by appearance). Races are not species; they are able to interbreed, and are fertile when they do. It is partly because such interbreeding has been quite frequent and has been continued over many centuries, that the notion of "pure races" is of course a myth. But this does not mean that different populations do not have different gene-pools which can be investigated, and which may serve to differentiate them.

Any taxonomy of races immediately runs into difficulties.

There are many different attempts to draw up a map of the different races of mankind, but they differ widely in the number of races recognized, and in the make-up of the particular races recognized. In 1775, Blumenbach, a contemporary of Linnaeus, put forward a system of classification in which men were categorized into Caucasians (white), Mongolians (yellow), Ethiopians (black), Malayans (brown), and Americans (red). This common-sense system, still widely popular among laymen, was entirely based on skin color. Since then, it has become possible to make use of advances in what is known as serological genetics to make more objective and quantitative analyses. In this method, specific genes can be recognized by chemical reactions with the components of human blood, and even as late as 1950 such serological analyses gave rise to races not noticeably different from those recognized by Blumenbach. Nevertheless, there is implicit in these new methods a great conceptual advance. We do not think of races as immutable types, each possessing certain qualities which are not present in the others, but rather as groups or populations which differ by the fact that various qualities are present in them in measurably different proportions.

The constant discovery of new blood-genes has forced experts to increase the number of races so recognized. However, morphological characteristics (that is, exterior appearances) are still widely used, and a widely accepted system (proposed by Dobzhansky in his book, *Mankind Evolving*) ends up with thirty-four. These are named, and their approximate locations noted, in Figure 2. But even this number still falls short of the observed number of sub-populations which can be shown to be different according to the definition we have adopted. Thus there are significant local variations within a country (even a small one, like Italy or Wales) which could be designated as races. If these are accepted then we have not five or six races, and not thirty or thirty-four, but literally thousands. How can we reconcile these many different estimates? An acceptable answer is given by I.I. Gottesman, in *Social Class, Race, and Psychological Development.*

"The apparent disagreements among taxonomists can be almost completely resolved by applying the term race at three different levels according to the purpose of the investigator. The first level describes the largest unit observed and is termed a geographical race; it corresponds with the races recognized by Blumenbach. There are no more than ten geographical races at the present time. Each such race comprises a collection of populations within geographical limits bounded by formerly insurmountable barriers to out-breeding, such as deserts, oceans, and mountains. Each shares a degree of homogeneity for blood-group genes and some morphological features, but still retains a considerable degree of heterogeneity for various characteristics. Some examples of geographical races are the Amerindians ranging from Alaska to Tierra del Fuego, with very low incidences of the genes for Type B blood and Rh-negative blood (r), and the African geographical race which occupies sub-Sahara Africa and which is characterized by extremely high frequency of the rhesus group gene R^0 and of the sickling gene associated with a type of anemia. The presence of blood-group genes is easily inferred from chemical tests that clot samples of blood.

A second level of usage of the term race is local race. This term is necessitated by the fact that subordinate to a geographical race are the different breeding populations themselves, the groups which anthropologists and geneticists study when they speak of a sample of Navajos, Bantu, or Eskimos. Local races may be separated by physical or social obstacles, they mate chiefly within their group (endogamy), and they are most like their nearest neighbors in gene frequencies. They number in the hundreds as contrasted with the six to ten geographical races, even though only

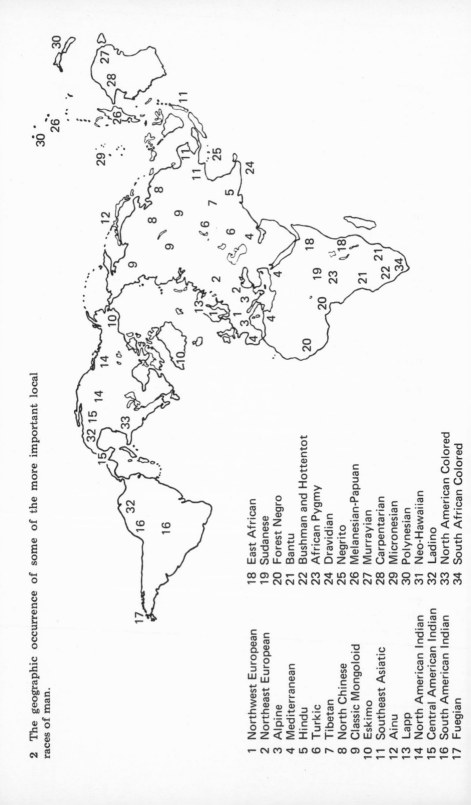

2 The geographic occurrence of some of the more important local races of man.

1 Northwest European
2 Northeast European
3 Alpine
4 Mediterranean
5 Hindu
6 Turkic
7 Tibetan
8 North Chinese
9 Classic Mongoloid
10 Eskimo
11 Southeast Asiatic
12 Ainu
13 Lapp
14 North American Indian
15 Central American Indian
16 South American Indian
17 Fuegian
18 East African
19 Sudanese
20 Forest Negro
21 Bantu
22 Bushman and Hottentot
23 African Pygmy
24 Dravidian
25 Negrito
26 Melanesian-Papuan
27 Murrayian
28 Carpentarian
29 Micronesian
30 Polynesian
31 Neo-Hawaiian
32 Ladino
33 North American Colored
34 South African Colored

thirty-four are singled out in Figure 2 as representative of the utility of the concept.

Even when looking at the genetic characteristics of a local race, one can observe significant pockets of variation. The populations are statistically distinct from neighboring pockets in some gene frequencies in the absence of geographical barriers or extensive cultural prohibitions. With high population density, mating tends to occur as a function of distance. Future geneticists may have to take note of the routes of buses and subway systems to understand their data. This phenomenon gives rise to our final level for the race concept, which is termed micro-geographical race or micro race to avoid confusion with the first level above. An example of micro races, which number in the thousands, is provided by a survey of blood types for the ABO blood groups in Wales. There were significant local variations in the gene frequencies even though Wales is a small country. If the maps included lines of communication for the past few centuries, they might add to our understanding of the formation of micro races."

Gottesman concludes his discussion by saying: "Race naming may be somewhat arbitary, but race differences are facts of nature which can be studies to help us understand the continuing evolution of man."

WITHIN THIS SET of concepts, where does the American Negro stand? It is often denied that American Negroes are in fact a race, on the grounds that they are not a pure race, having interbred with whites for several hundred years. But that is not an acceptable argument; as we have seen, the term race implies genetic differences between two recognisable groups in terms of gene pools, and makes no implications about purity. Pure races do not exist, but impure ones do. This is not to say that American Negroes are necessarily like African Negroes; it is a question of fact whether these are now two races, or one. It is also a question of fact whether or not American Negroes living in the south are similar to those living in the north, or whether in fact there are several sub-races to be recognized even within the confines of the U.S.A. These are important questions, because, as we shall see, we cannot at the moment make any useful generalizations about inherited mental ability for populations as culturally diverse as European and American whites, or African blacks. They are much closer to being answerable when we consider American whites and American Negroes, sharing a common cultural heritage and a common educational system—at least to a point where meaningful comparisons can be made, and meaningful experiments carried out. Whether the similarities are sufficient to make the deductions convincing is a question we shall have to turn to later. North American Negroes are certainly hybrids, and when in what follows we refer to "Negroes" without qualification, this term will be used for this hybrid race resident in the U.S.A. and recognizable by various morphological features.

The majority of slaves appear to have come from the west coast of Africa, not much more than two hundred miles inland; Pollitzer's map of Africa, reproduced as Figure 3, shows the origins of some 72,000 slaves imported from 1733 to 1807. It is important to know the true habitat of these forefathers of modern American Negroes, as estimates of the degree of hybridization which has taken place is based entirely on knowledge of the gene frequencies of the present inhabitants of these areas. The best available estimates suggest an admixture of about 25 to 30% of white genes in present-day Negroes in the U.S.A. It is calculated that it would take some 120 generations to make the two gene pools equal, assuming the present amount of interbreeding (or rather the estimated amount of interbreeding which has been going on over the past ten generations).

It is not suggested that Negroes all over the U.S.A. are uniform in the admixture of white genes; the evidence on this

3 African origins of the slaves imported to Charleston from 1733 to 1807. The dots indicate the main areas from which slaves were imported.

1 Egypt
2 Libya
3 Algeria
4 Morocco
5 Spanish Sahara
6 Senegal
7 French West Africa
8 French Guinea
9 Sierra Leone
10 Liberia
11 Ivory Coast
12 Gold Coast
13 Dahomey
14 Nigeria
15 Cameroons
16 French Equatorial Africa

17 Anglo-Egyptian Sudan
18 Eritrea
19 Ethiopia
20 Belgian Congo
21 Moanda
22 Kenya
23 Tanganyika
24 R.U.
25 Angola
26 Northern Rhodesia
27 Mozambique
28 Southern Rhodesia
29 South West Africa
30 Bechuanaland
31 South Africa

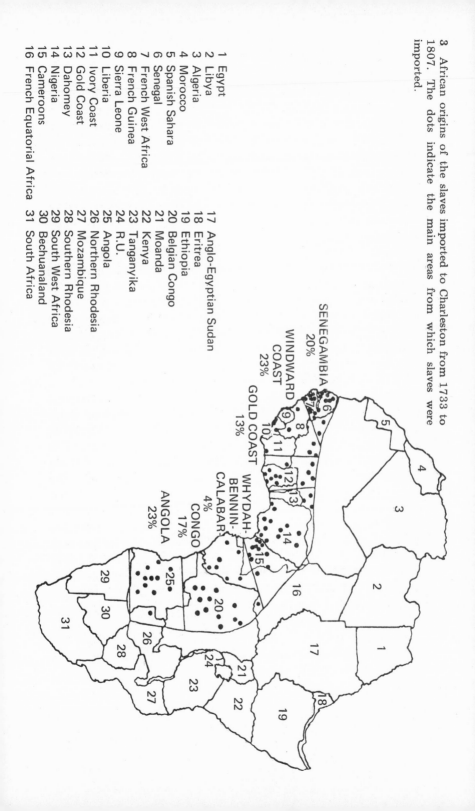

point is quite strong. Pollitzer estimated the "biological distance" between groups of West African Negroes, U.S. Negroes living near Charleston (the former great importation center for slaves), non-Charleston U.S. Negroes, and U.S. whites. He used two different bases of estimation: nine morphological and fifteen serological characteristics. The results are shown in Figure 4. It will be clear that Charleston Negroes are much more like their West African forefathers than are Negroes from further north, who are much closer to the whites in both respects than are the Charleston Negroes. We are thus not really justified in talking about "American blacks" as if they were a uniform population with similar shares in a general gene pool. However, these facts are not really too relevant to any discussion of possible genetic influences on racial differences in intelligence. If Negroes tend to have lower IQ's, in part on a genetic basis, then the admixture of white genes would if anything have reduced the observed difference. If this were true, then it would seem to follow that low IQ's should be found more consistently in those Negro subsamples which on morphological and serological grounds were closer to the West-African type, *i.e.* those living in the southern states. We shall see presently whether or not this deduction can be verified.

It is a curious fact that we tend to label a person "Negro" if there is any trace of Negro ancestry in his background, or if his morphological characteristics suggest such a trace. Gottesman points out how illogical this procedure is. As we have seen, northern Negroes have something like 25% of white genes; this corresponds roughly to having a white grandfather. "If you choose to call the white individual with a Negro grandfather a Negro, then logic would require you to call the 'average' Negro in New York or Baltimore white. The science of human genetics cannot tell you whom to call Negro or white; it can only provide the biological facts as we now know them." In other words, we are dealing with a continuum from white to black, not with two sharply distinguished populations, and serological and morphological analysis can tell us roughly where on this continuum a given person is located. Instead of this, we prefer to take one end of this continuum and call it "white"; every person who is found to be (or suspected of being) anywhere else on the continuum we call black, very much as Hitler called everyone a "Jew" among whose ancestors there could be traced someone, however remote, who had been a member of this particular religious group.

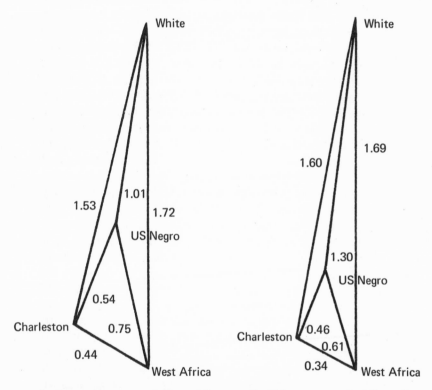

4 Schematic representation of the genetic distances among white and Negro populations. The left-hand diagram is based on morphology, the right on serology.

It has puzzled many people that genetically different sub-groups of *homo sapiens* should be found on this earth. A good answer can be found in an experiment reported by Dobzhansky, who took ten groups of twenty fruit flies from a fairly heterogenous population. These groups were maintained under uniform conditions for some eighteen months, which was equal to twenty generations. The final descendants, numbering from one to four thousand animals, were very divergent genetically. Without knowledge of the conditions of the experiment, no one would have suspected them to have come from the same stock. Twenty generations, in human terms, equals a period of less than six hundred years. If random samples of human beings had been chosen in a similar haphazard fashion and dispersed into quite similar but non-communicating environments, their offspring after the passage of this amount of time would show similar genetic dissimilarities, due to genetic drift accompanied by natural selection.* As an example of the way in which gene frequencies in different populations can be determined by natural selection, consider sicklecell anaemia.

THIS DISORDER is determined by a recessive gene. If a given person receives it from both his parents, it will probably prove lethal before he reaches maturity, and he will die of anaemia. Individuals who only receive the trait from one parent will be carriers, but themselves free of the disease, and it also happens that they are particularly resistant to malaria. So the disadvantages of the disease when inherited from both parents (death from anaemia and so failure to reproduce) are counterblanced by the advantages of inheritance from one parent only (avoidance of death from

*Genetic drift is a term used to refer to changes in gene frequency in small breeding populations due to chance fluctuations. Natural selection—that is, the preponderance of those gene-types best adapted to the prevailing environmental conditions—exerts a directive influence on the process.

malaria). The sickling trait would constitute an advantage only in an environment in which malaria was a frequent source of debility. Elsewhere it would be eliminated through natural selection not counter-balanced by any such advantages. Among Negro tribes in Africa, 20%, and on occasion even 40%, of the population have the sickling trait. Among Charleston Negroes the frequency is about 16%, and in other American Negro samples it is between 7% and 10%. Some of this reduction in trait frequency is due to hybridization; but in the main it is probably due to the failure of the gene to be adaptive in a non-malarial environment.

Similar adaptive advantages probably account for morphological differences more easily observed. Darker skin color protects from sunburn and radiation, and is known to decrease the probability of skin cancer, while white skin color may be advantageous in increasing the production of Vitamin D when winters are long and skies overcast. There are, thus, many reasons for believing that the general causes of the origins and continuations of racial differences are beginning to be understood. As Gottesman says, "genetic racial differences are facts of nature and not signs of inferiority or superiority in themselves. Differences observed appear to be, for the most part, the results of selection for adaptation to ancient or contemporary environmental diversity, especially climatic and disease factors." . . . It would be idle to pretend that we know more than we do; but it would be equally idle to pretend, as many sociologists and others remote from these inquiries do, that nothing is known. Mathematical methods of assessing interracial distances, along the lines of Figure 4, are being worked out and perfected; and while, again, it should not be assumed that everything that needs to be known is in fact known, we are constantly advancing towards a better understanding of race, and a better description of the dimensions involved.

When we turn to intelligence, it may seem paradoxical that selection should ever favor the less intelligent, and consequently it may be difficult to reconcile the theories presented above with the possibility of any given racial group having lower genetic potential than others. Yet it is easy to consider such possibilities. If, for instance, the brighter members of the West African tribes which suffered the depredations of the slavers had managed to use their higher intelligence to escape, so that it was mostly the duller ones who got caught, then the gene pool of the slaves brought to America would have been depleted of many high-IQ genes. Alternatively, many slaves appear to have been sold by their tribal chiefs; these chiefs might have got rid of their less intelligent followers. And as far as natural selection after the shipment to America is concerned, it is quite possible that the more intelligent Negroes would have contributed an undue proportion of "uppity" slaves, as well as being much more likely to try and escape. The terrible fate of slaves falling into either of these categories is only too well known. White slavers wanted dull beasts of burden, ready to work themselves to death in the plantations, and under those conditions intelligence would have been counter-selective. Thus there is every reason to expect that the particular sub-sample of the Negro race which is constituted of American Negroes is not an unselected sample of Negroes, but has been selected throughout history according to criteria which would put the highly intelligent at a disadvantage. The inevitable outcome of such selection would of course be the creation of a gene pool lacking some of the genes making for higher intelligence.

THESE ARGUMENTS should not be taken too far. It is possible, and may even be likely, that these counter-selective trends may have taken place; we cannot be certain. Too little is known about the precise nature of slave raids, and of later within-group selection, to be certain of anything. Stories and anecdotes may be suggestive, but they cannot give us the needed facts. Particularly, the absence of IQ tests at the time makes any conclusions suspect. Thus all we can say is that even if there are no genetic differences in ability between Negroes in general and whites, it is not impossible that American Negroes may be the descendants of a highly selected sample of African Negroes less bright than the total group. It is known that many other groups came to the U.S.A. due to pressures which made them very poor samples of the original populations. Italians, Spaniards, and Portuguese, as well as Greeks, are examples where the less able, less intelligent were forced through circumstances to emigrate, and where their American progeny showed significantly lower IQ's than would have been shown by a random sample of the original population. Other groups, like the Irish, probably showed the opposite tendency; it was the more intelligent members of these groups who emigrated to the U.S.A., leaving their less intelligent brethren behind. Thus the observed IQ differences of racial and national groups inside the U.S.A., even if they could be accounted for in part on genetic grounds, would be no guide at all to the level of intelligence of the much larger groups of which they present a non-random sample. This is true of the various European nations which have been studied in this manner, and it is equally true of the Negro population. We can speculate, but there is no way of knowing.

3
WHAT IS INTELLIGENCE?

MOST ADULTS, and practically all children in this country, are now at least vaguely familiar with the term "IQ" or Intelligence Quotient. This is a measure derived from intelligence tests and purports to measure a person's standing on a continuum ranging from low to high, with a mean defined as 100. Figure 5 shows the general shape of distribution of IQ's around this mean value of 100. It will be seen that less than ½% have IQ's less than 60, or higher than 140, with 50% between 90 and 110. Actually this "normal" curve is somewhat misleading. There is a "hump" between 50 and 60, where low IQ's due to birth injury accumulate, and there appears to be an excess of high IQ's (above 140) the reason for which is not known. The term IQ was derived from an actual quotient: mental age divided by chronological age, usually multiplied by 100 to get rid of decimal points; mental age in this quotient represented the age level which was represented by an individual child's actual performance, irrespective of his actual (chronological) age. Thus a child of eight who performed on an intelligent test at the level of a "typical" (average) twelve-year-old had a mental age of twelve. As mental age does not increase beyond sixteen or thereabouts, the term really has no application for adults; but it is still used although the values of IQ are now more frequently determined by direct statistical means, rather than

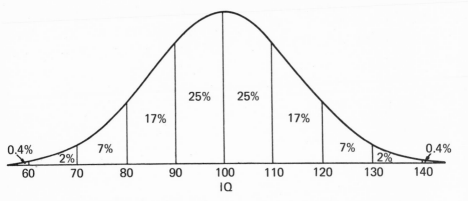

5a Normal curve of disribution of intelligence, showing the expected percentages of the population in each IQ range. Except at the extremes, these percentages are quite close to what occur in actual populations.

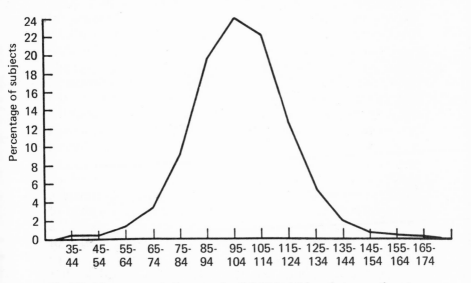

5b IQs of a representative sample of 2,904 children between the ages of 2 and 18, showing the percentage of subjects whose scores fall into each five-point interval. The IQs are based on Stanford-Binet tests.

What Is Intelligence?

by any kind of division. IQ's thus present a convenient method for comparing results on different tests; but we need to be very careful about their statistical meaning if we are to avoid misinterpretations.

The question which is always asked by laymen and students when this topic is introduced is: *"How do you know that your tests measure intelligence?"* And the objection which is often advanced against IQ testing by more sophisticated critics is: "Surely you are reifying intelligence —treating it as if it were a thing."

These two well-known points cancel out, in a sense. To ask how we know that we are measuring intelligence is to reify intelligence; we are being asked, in effect, how we know that our measurements stack up against something existing outside these measurements. This, of course, is an impossible question. You might just as well ask how we know that we measure gravitation, or heat, or any other physical concept. The answer is that certain concepts emerge from our scientific study of the particular universe of phenomena in which we are interested. Our measures are geared to our understanding of these phenomena, and incorporate these theories. Intelligence is not a "thing," but a concept—just as gravitation is a concept, or heat. And the accusation that psychologists tend to "reify" intelligence is simply not true, although our habitual methods of speaking and writing may often make it appear so. It is often awkward to rephrase simple sentences to avoid giving the impression that intelligence is a "thing"; but then readers familiar with the field are well aware of the precise implications of the terms used.

THIS LEADS US to another point which is often misunderstood. Concepts like intelligence are defined in terms of a general theoretical network, and within this network they are given "operational definition" in terms of some kind of measurement. Gravitation is a concept we arrive at by measuring certain properties in a network that includes falling apples and circling planets: this is its operational definition. The same is true of intelligence, and the often-used answer *"Intelligence is what intelligence tests measure"* is neither an attempt to avoid the question nor a mere tautology. In a very real sense the question "What is electricity?" can be answered by enumerating the experiments we use to measure electricity. Electricity is that which heats a wire when passing through it; it is that which turns a magnetic needle when passing over it; it is that which makes iron magnetic when passing around it. Many years after Faraday's great work, and Maxwell's theoretical and mathematical labors, we have a theory which we can offer the inquirer, and which he may find more satisfying, but it is doubtful if Faraday, Ampere, and Ohm would have offered him anything beyond a statement that electricity was what electricity tests measure. The tautology of such a statement is only apparent. Faraday was much concerned with the problem, for instance, of whether there was only one kind of electricity, or five. Quite different results would have been found in making these simple measurements if Faraday had been wrong, and there had been more than one kind of electricity. Similarly, measurements of heat preceded good theories of heat; early efforts were literally based on the sensations of hot and cold felt by people when exposed to a fire, or snow, and attempts were made to find physical phenomena which would correspond to these subjective sensations.

Naturally we wish to go beyond such operational definitions, and indeed even operational definitions usually incorporate a theory, even though it may not be clearly expressed. Such a definition was presented by Spearman when he defined intelligence as *"the ability to educe relations and correlates"*; or even earlier when St. Thomas Aquinas called intelligence *"the ability to combine and separate."* Both definitions emphasize the processes of abstraction and

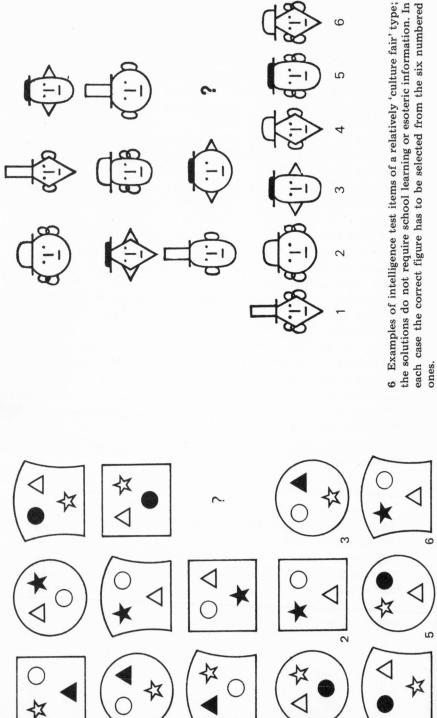

6 Examples of intelligence test items of a relatively 'culture fair' type; the solutions do not require school learning or esoteric information. In each case the correct figure has to be selected from the six numbered ones.

conceptualization. Aquinas based his view on common sense, philosophical deliberation, and observation; Spearman relied more on specially constructed tests and objectively calculated relations between the scores made on these tests by thousands of school children. He empirically verified a number of deductions from his theory that there was only one general factor of intelligence. Thus he discovered if one takes a random sample of the population and administers various intelligence tests, the results of these different tests correlate positively with each other. (In other words, they appear to be measuring the same thing.) He also found that different tests measure this common underlying ability with greater or lesser success, and that this success depends on the conformity of the test to his hypothesis. Thus matrix-type tests, illustrated in Figure 6, always have very high correlations with abstract intelligence, being almost pure examples of the "ability to educe relations and correlates." He probably underestimated the importance of the form in which the test was presented, and the material used (verbal, perceptual, numerical). It has been found that these influences give rise to various sub-factors (verbal ability, numerical ability, perceptual ability, etc.) But on the whole, although we do not any longer use the precise language which Spearman used, and although other theories are still under consideration, the facts have strongly borne out his main contentions. Even if we only consider his general intelligence, or "*g*," as an average of many different "group" or "primary" ability factors, nevertheless this average ability determines to a considerable extent our success or failure in the educational field. Furthermore, such "primary abilities" are usually found to be themselves correlated, often quite highly, and these intercorrelations in turn give rise to something very much like Spearman's "*g*." There is no point here and now in entering into a complex consideration of the many different questions which have arisen in this field. The empirical data strongly support, and nowhere refute, the notion that our problem-solving behavior in a great variety of different situations can be accounted for, as far as individual differences are concerned, by reference to a concept of general intelligence which is reasonably well measured by traditional intelligence tests.

In thinking about IQ tests, most people get confused by a question which is indeed central to one's understanding, but which is not as difficult as it may often seem. The question I have in mind is the cultural content of the tests. These are supposed to measure intelligence, but to many people they seem to contain so much material which is obviously learned, and may be peculiar to a particular culture, that it might seem more appropriate to call these tests measures of education. The format may be unusual, but the contents often call for knowledge, rather than Spearman's "education of relations and correlates." Take two examples:

A *Black is to white as high is to:*
        green tall low grey
B *Jupiter is to Mars as Zeus is to:*
        Poseidon Ares Apollo Hermes

Clearly the form of the two items is identical, and calls for the education of a relation; in example A that of "oppositeness," in B that of Roman to Greek gods. But while A is a proper intelligence test item in that all persons likely to encounter it are familiar with the fundaments (black, white, high, low, etc.) B is unlikely to meet this criterion—not every schoolboy (in spite of Macaulay's belief) would know classical mythology in sufficient detail to make this a test of anything but school knowledge. The eductive process in this case is merely a gloss; the crucial element is the acquired knowledge of ancient gods. Yet one might say that in A, also, there is an element of culture and school knowledge. A French or German boy would not know the English words, for instance, and a youngster who had not learned to read even in the most elementary fashion would not be able to do the test—nor would you expect a child to do well who had never been taught to write with a pencil. These examples are extreme; but they do illustrate that intelligence tests can never be viewed apart from a common cultural, educational heritage. Where this is missing, comparison becomes difficult if not impossible.

In this, of course, intelligence testing does not differ from measurement in other sciences. We have some understanding of temperature measurement through repeated use of thermometers; but our thermometers would not work very well near absolute zero or in the interior of the sun. Quite different types of apparatus are required to take care of conditions differing so markedly from those on earth. Similarly, we think that we understand intuitively the measurement of length; but (as we now know) this too is subject to Alice-in-Wonderland contractions when moving at a high speed. All measurement is relative, and we need neither be surprised nor upset because this is also true of psychological measurement. As long as the limitations are properly understood, we can work reasonably well within them. But we move outside them at our peril, and much of the controversy that has arisen in this field is due to an improper understanding of just what these limitations are.

MANY PEOPLE HAVE ARGUED that "culture free" intelligence tests are impossible, and that consequently any proper measurement of intelligence, and in particular any determination of the influence of heredity on individual differences in IQ, is impossible. The objection is valid, as we have seen; at the moment, there are no culture free tests.*

*This may not always remain so. There is now evidence that evoked potentials in the brain differ significantly in children who score high or low on IQ tests; high scores have potentials which are believed to signify quick processing of information. It may become possible, in due course, to measure intelligence in such physiological terms, using omnipresent stimuli like blips of light and brief sounds to trigger off the EEG (electroencephalograph). This is already possible to some extent: see Figure 7.

What we do have is a set of tests, or test items, graded from one end of a continuum where cultural factors are at a minimum ("culture fair") to the other end of the continuum where items are very heavily loaded with cultural factors. Items A and B in our example may serve to illustrate this difference. Another example would be to take on the one hand the items in Figure 6, which are pretty culture fair, and on the other the items from a typical "picture vocabulary" test, in which pictures of objects are shown and the testee has to pick out the correct word to describe the object; this test is very "culture bound." There is much agreement between psychologists about the degree to which tests are subject to cultural bias; and while it would be nice to have a perfectly culture free test, mathematical projection becomes possible the moment we are dealing with a continuum such as the "culture fair—culture determined" one described above.

But, many critics will say, such tests as are used in the typical educational selection test (such as the 11+ in England, which marked the end of the primary stage of education and, in part, determined allocation to different secondary schools or streams) are clearly not culture fair. They contain a large amount of material which is very heavily dependent on school instruction—so much so that many parents get into difficulties in trying to do the tests! This is true. But remember that these tests are *not* meant to be universally valid, nor to give as pure a measure of IQ as could be obtained. Their purpose is to predict which children will do well in grammar schools or in the advanced streams of other types of secondary or comprehensive schools; and experience has shown that pure IQ tests do this less well than do tests somewhat adulterated with school knowledge. Such tests are more properly called "verbal reasoning tests." They are not, and are not meant to be, pure IQ tests, even within the limits of purity which can be achieved. I happen to think that the wrong choice has in fact been made by the educationists who

7a "Brain waves" resulting from a sudden stimulus (light). The waves are the "evoked potentials" recorded on an electroencephalograph, and the score used is the wave length of the first four waves to occur (E^1 to E^4). Note that the wave lengths are shortest for the brightest, longest for the dullest subject. In other words, transmission of information is quick for bright, slow for dull subjects.

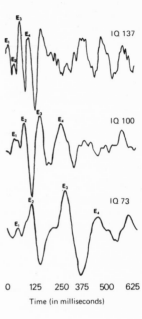

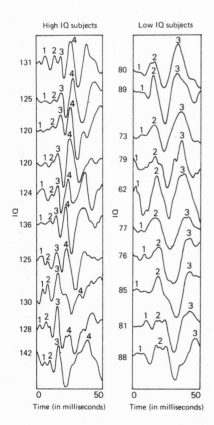

7b Evoked potentials from ten bright and ten dull subjects. Note the quick waves in the former, and the slow waves in the latter.

constructed these tests. If you want to measure two different things (IQ and school knowledge) then you should have two separate tests, so that you can mix these two different variables in the proportion that gives you the best prediction. But the choice is not up to psychologists, unfortunately; and it would be unreasonable to blame them for what is not their responsibility. (Not that this will prevent people from blaming them, of course!)

There is another complication. Bright children—as determined by culture fair tests—have been found to pick up knowledge (including school knowledge) much more rapidly than dull children. It follows that simple tests of knowledge, such as a vocabulary test or a general knowledge test, will in fact correlate quite highly with culture fair tests. This is only true under conditions of universal, compulsory education; but if you take a country like England, this is what countless investigations have shown. Cattell distinguishes between *fluid* and *crystallized* intelligence—meaning by this the distinction between ability for new conceptual learning and problem solving, and acquired knowledge and developed intellectual skills. Most tests measure both, in varying proportions; and, of course, in the vast majority of people the two are highly correlated. With age, fluid ability decreases, while crystallized ability stays much the same, or may even increase. Clearly, fluid ability is more closely allied with culture fair tests, and it is with this ability that we shall mostly be concerned.

IS THIS INTELLIGENCE important? Critics have often played down IQ as relatively unimportant and even irrelevant. But this would seem to be a mistake. It would be an equally serious mistake to regard it as all-important. Clearly there is more to life than problem solving or abstract ability. Neither is it reasonable to pronounce a person generally inferior—or superior—on the grounds of his IQ. The poor, dull Negro mother working out her guts to keep her family together is, in human terms, worth many times such bright world conquerors as Alexander, Napoleon, Hitler, Stalin or Mussolini. There are many human qualities quite uncorrelated with IQ, such as courage, compassion, friendliness, "soul," and helpfulness, just as there are many abilities, particularly in the arts, which are only marginally correlated with IQ. Nobody has ever suggested that a measurement of IQ appraises the general worth of a person.

But all this does not mean that what IQ tests measure is unimportant. If you grade occupations in order of dependence on intellectual ability, from high to low, you will find that this order correlates almost perfectly with the prestige of the occupations, and also with the socio-economic status of those engaged in them. Our society values highly the abilities measured by IQ tests, our educational system is such that those who score highly are also found to do best, on the whole, in their examinations, and those who are successful in the more complex and difficult jobs are usually those who score well on IQ tests. This is not only true in England and the U.S.A.; it was also found to be true in the U.S.S.R. (so much so that Stalin decreed that intelligence testing had to stop—the results went against the doctrine of Communist egalitarianism and the myth of omnipotent "Soviet man").

There is a large literature showing that intelligence as measured by IQ tests does make for success in almost any undertaking which requires intellectual application, the learning of complex material or the assimilation of new information. This is true even where one might have expected IQ to play only a minor part, as in officer selection. Bright applicants make better officers; this was discovered in the U.S.A. during the First World War, and verified in the UK during the Second. One might have thought that non-intellectual qualities, like courage or care for the soldiers under one's command, would have been far more important. Yet the results of large-scale testing are quite clear in demonstrating that IQ tests predict officer success better than any other tests, and certainly far better than any interview procedures.

Prediction in the educational field is of course very much better than in other fields, if only because education is almost entirely geared to intellectual ability. It is not, of course, suggested, that IQ tests predict perfectly how well the child will do at school, or the adolescent at college. Obviously there are many other factors which come into the picture, such as motivation, parental help, financial difficulties, and emotional entanglements. What the figures show is simply that absence of a given level of intellectual ability (low IQ) is an almost absolute bar to progress towards higher education (as well as being usually coupled with a dislike of further education, and a strong desire to get out of school and earn a living!) University students in Great Britain have an average IQ of 125 or so; anyone with an IQ below 115 or so is not likely to get into a university in the first place, and he is certainly not likely to graduate even if he should surmount the admission hurdle. Nor is he likely to enjoy his stay.*

A well-known study carried out at the London School of Economics will illustrate the importance of IQ. Prospective students were interviewed along traditional lines by a Senior Tutor, with special attention to the likelihood, on personal and intellectual grounds, of their succeeding in completing their courses. This interview determined their acceptance or rejection. Those accepted were also given psychological tests, the results of which were not made known to anyone until the students in question had either graduated (with good or poor honors) or failed. Predictions made by the interviewers (all very experienced at the job) had zero predictive accuracy. The tests predicted future success quite well. Actually, the

*Students with high IQ's may or may not succeed; this depends on many other factors, such as those named. It also depends on their choice of subject; special abilities may be vital for success in specialized subjects, provided the IQ is high enough.

accuracy of the interview was probably much lower than zero, *i.e.* negative; interviewers had available headmasters' reports and other material about the candidate's past career, as well as some essays he had written, and this material by itself gave quite a reasonable prediction, although not as good as the IQ tests. The interview by itself must have lowered the predictive value of all the material available to the interviewer until a zero prediction accuracy was reached; thus the value of the interview as such must be assessed as being roughly −0.3 in terms of correlation with terminal performance. (It is hardly necessary to tell the reader that as a consequence the LSE refused to have any truck with IQ tests, and continued the demonstrably useless interviewing procedure. Perhaps the troubles which ensued with their students are not unrelated to this decision!)

We conclude that IQ tests measure important intellectual qualities in children and adults; that these qualities are very important both in education and in professions and jobs requiring abilities for abstract thinking and problem solving; and that while such tests cannot be culture free, they can be culture fair to varying degrees.

CAN WE SAY ANYTHING useful about the vexed problem of the degree to which differences in IQ are due to genetic causes? The answer is yes; and indeed if we restrict ourselves, as we must, to given populations at a given time in history, there is much agreement that heredity plays a very important part indeed in causing such differences. The best available estimates suggest a ratio of 4 to 1 for the relative importance of the contributions of heredity and environment. In other words, genetic factors are responsible for something like 80% of all the variation which we find in IQ's within a given population such as that living in England or the U.S.A. at the present time. It is not suggested that this figure would apply necessarily to other countries at the present time, or to those countries at other times in the past, or in the future; such

TABLE 1

Correlations between	Number of Studies	Obtained Median r*	Theoretical Value[1]	Theoretical Value[2]
Unrelated persons				
Children reared apart	4	−.01	.00	.00
Foster parent and child	3	+.20	.00	.00
Children reared together	5	+.24	.00	.00
Collaterals				
Second cousins	1	+.16	+ .14	+ .063
First cousins	3	+.26	+ .18	+ .125
Uncle (or aunt) and nephew (or niece)	1	+.34	+ .31	+ .25
Siblings, reared apart	33	+.47	+ .52	+ .50
Siblings, reared together	36	+.55	+ .52	+ .50
Dizygotic twins, different sex	9	+.49	+ .50	+ .50
Dizygotic twins, same sex	11	+.56	+ .54	+ .50
Monozygotic twins, reared apart	4	+.75	+1.00	+1.00
Monozygotic twins, reared together	14	+.87	+1.00	+1.00
Direct line				
Grandparent and grandchild	3	+.27	+ .31	+ .25
Parent (as adult) and child	13	+.50	+ .49	+ .50
Parent (as child) and child	1	+.56	+ .49	+ .50

*Correlations not corrected for attenuation (unreliability)
[1] Assuming assortative mating and partial dominance
[2] Assuming random mating and only additive genes, *i.e.,* the simplest possible polygenic model

This table compares the correlation of IQ among people related to each other in various ways with the correlation one would expect to find if differences in IQ were completely determined by heredity. The table summarizes well over 100 studies and is taken from Jensen's monograph. The most appropriate comparison is between the column stating the *"Obtained Median r"* and that giving the "Theoretical Value 1" assuming assorative mating and partial dominance. It will be seen that agreement is pretty good, although of course far from perfect. The degree of imperfection of fit between the theoretical model and the actual figures can be used to calculate the amount of environmental influence that must be postulated, and this calculation gives us the value of 20% or thereabouts.

figures are strictly relative to a particular environment, and are subject to change. In particular, the more egalitarian our educational system becomes, the greater will be the influence of genetic factors. By equating environmental influences which might affect IQ, we increase the importance of genetic determinants. This is an interesting, and perhaps unexpected, result of the work of egalitarian political movements whose preference would be very much for an entirely environmentalistic determination of IQ.

The evidence for the 4:1 ratio between genetic and environmental influences is well enough known to be mentioned only in passing. It rests essentially on studies of similarity in IQ between members of the same family, on the one hand, and on studies of IQ under conditions where environment can be controlled, on the other.

Table 1, for example, shows a comparison between the similarity of IQ's among a number of people having various family relationships to each other, and the similarity one would expect if IQ were determined entirely by heredity. Such familiar studies—including particularly the very important investigation of identical twins reared apart—have often used IQ tests less "culture fair" than desirable, and in consequence it seems likely that a repetition with a better choice of test might increase the value of IQ heritability beyond 80%.

In these studies the degree of genetic similarity is known, and the environment is random. In other studies, direct measurement of environmental "goodness" is undertaken, and correlated with the IQ of children brought up in this environment. (Usually foster children are employed in such studies in order to avoid the contamination of environmental with genetic factors. It is essential, of course, that the adoption agency should not be placing the children selectively.) In a famous study on these lines Burks spent between four and eight hours in investigating each adoptive home, very carefully rating all environmental variables which had been suggested as possibly relevant to the determination of high IQ's. He included the adopting parents' intelligence as part of the children's environment, as well as such factors as the amount of time the parents spent helping the children with their school work, the amount of time spent reading to them, and so on. The proportion of IQ variance accounted for by all these environmental factors combined was 18%, which agrees well with the figure of 80% for the influence of heredity; the two add up to just about 100%. It should perhaps be added that the population sampled in this study was broadly representative of the American white environments, excluding only perhaps an extreme 5%; thus it cannot be said that these results are due to lack of variability in environmental determinants.

A third type of study, also very important, is one in which environmental variation is kept to a minimum. This is achieved in orphanages where, with respect to educationally relevant experiences, all children are treated as exactly alike as is humanly possible. With children who come to such orphanages shortly after birth, it seems reasonable to expect that their variability in IQ would be much reduced if environment had much to do with the creation of IQ differences. This is not, in fact, found. The variability of orphanage children is reduced very little below that observed in the outer world. This is clearly incompatible with a strong environmentalist doctrine. Thus the manipulation of the environment gives us much the same answer as the careful study of different degrees of genetic similarity; heredity plays an extremely important part in the genesis of IQ differences. The direct study of environmental influences discloses them to be rather slight, and to add up to no more than something like 20%.

It is interesting to note that tests of school achievement show evidence of much lower heritability than do measures of IQ. Results are variable, as one might expect, depending on the actual tests used, the populations studied, and so forth. But the degree to which achievement depends on heredity, as suggested by tests of this kind, is at most half that demonstrated for IQ, and usually it is much less. Critics who declare that IQ tests are simply tests of scholastic achievement seldom stay to demonstrate how it is possible, if the two types of test are identical in nature, that IQ tests come out with 80% heritability and school knowledge tests with 40% heritability or less. Clearly there are vital differences between the two. The lower degree of heritability of the school knowledge tests is precisely what one would expect if the acquisition of such knowledge was determined in part by intelligence, in part by other, environmental influences which did not affect intelligence itself to anything like the same extent.

I will not discuss the arguments often presented by sociologists in an effort to minimize the impact of these figures, mainly because these arguments seem to rest on an inability to follow the detail of the experimental and statistical treatment involved. Let me just give an example which is typical of the sort of contradictory reasoning often employed in this field.

We have noted Burks' famous study of the influence of environmental factors, carefully measured and correlated. Some critics have suggested that perhaps the "true" environmental factors involved are much more subtle than those studied and measured by Burks, though they have not made clear just what those factors might be. But contrast this with the criticisms made, often by the same people, of the identical twin studies where the twins were reared in separation from each other. The result of these studies has been that there is not very much difference between the twins, and certainly not much more difference than between identical twins brought up together. This leads to the criticism that the environments of the twins brought up in separation were not so very different. Using crude indices, it can indeed be shown that extremes of poverty or affluence

TABLE 2 Distribution of intelligence according to occupational class: adults.

IQ	Professional Higher I	Lower II	Clerical III	Skilled IV	Semi-skilled V	Unskilled VI	Total
50–60						1	1
60–70					5	18	23
70–80				2	15	52	69
80–90			1	11	31	117	160
90–100			8	51	135	53	247
100–110			16	101	120	11	248
110–120		2	56	78	17	9	162
120–130		13	38	14	2		67
130–140	2	15	3	1			21
140+	1	1					2
Total	3	31	122	258	325	261	1000
Mean IQ	139.7	130.6	115.9	108.2	97.8	84.9	100

++++++++++

TABLE 3 Distribution of intelligence according to occupational class: children.

IQ	Professional Higher I	Lower II	Clerical III	Skilled IV	Semi-skilled V	Unskilled VI	Total
50–60					1	1	2
60–70				1	6	15	22
70–80			3	12	23	32	70
80–90		1	8	33	55	62	159
90–100		2	21	53	99	75	250
100–110	1	6	31	70	85	54	247
110–120		12	35	59	38	16	160
120–130	1	8	18	22	13	6	68
130–140	1	2	6	7	5		21
140+				1			1
Total	3	31	122	258	325	261	1000
Mean IQ	120.8	114.7	107.8	104.6	98.9	92.6	100

The data in these two tables were collected by Sir Cyril Burt on some 40,000 adults and children and have been reduced to a base of 1,000. (This means that the total of 3 for the higher professional category actually refers to 120 fathers.)

are not often found in this connection. But different the environments certainly were; and if we can postulate such factors as have been called in to criticize the Burks study, how can we now turn around and adopt exactly the opposite point of view, asserting that differences which are supposed to exist even within a single family do not exist between families?*

There is one further interesting source of information which is relevant both to the genetic argument and also to our contention that intelligence is correlated with the intellectual demands of a given occupation. Table 2 shows the distribution of intelligence according to occupational class. Average IQ's range from 140 for the higher professional group to 85 for the unskilled workers; it will also be noticed that there is a fair degree of overlap, particularly between adjacent groups. Table 3 gives similar data for the children of fathers in these various professional groups.

It will be noticed that something very interesting has taken place. We now have regression to the mean; the children of our higher professional fathers have a mean IQ of only 121, that is, they have regressed half way to the mean of the whole population, which is of course 100. Similarly, the children of the unskilled parents have an IQ of 93; they have regressed upwards and roughly half way towards the population mean. This *regression to the mean* is a phenomenon well known in genetics, and characteristic of traits

*That the criticism is without value can be shown by looking at the actual homes of the separated identical twins studied by Sir Cyril Burt. He classified parents' or foster parents' occupations on a six-point scale, ranging from *(1)* higher professional through *(2)* lower professional, *(3)* clerical, *(4)* skilled and *(5)* semi-skilled to *(6)* unskilled. The correlation between the socio-economic status of the home in which the one twin was brought up correlated 0.03 with that in which the other twin was brought up! In other words, there was considerable diversity in socio-economic status between homes, and the environment in which one of the twins was brought up bore no more than a chance relation to that in which the other one was brought up.

markedly influenced by genetic causes. Environment would favor the children of the higher professional fathers, and disfavor those of unskilled working-class fathers, tending to make the difference between them even greater than that observed between their fathers. Clearly this is *not* what happens. Regression presents strong evidence for genetic determination of IQ differences. Regression also implies that if the next generation (that is, the children in the sample studied by Burt) take up occupations which correlate with their IQ's in the same way that their fathers' did, then a considerable change-over in social class must occur. Burt calculates that something like a 30% change-over does in fact occur, with the brighter children of the lower-class parents rising into the higher social strata, and the duller children of the higher-class parents falling into lower social strata. Again, intelligence is of course not the only variable relevant to this change; but it is clearly and indisputably a very important one. It has been suggested that in the U.S.A. the amount of social mobility is even greater, producing a closer approximation to a "meritocracy" than would be tolerated by the "old school tie" culture still dominating England.

What do those who deny the importance of genetic determinants in the causation of individual differences in intelligence reply to the argument from regression? The answer to this is twofold. Most environmentalists do not reply to it at all because they disregard this rather astonishing fact completely. Those who do pay some attention to it argue along lines which may at first seem reasonable, but which can be seen to be contradictory. They say that the fact that fathers are highly intelligent and occupationally success-ful does not guarantee an optimum upbringing for their children. Other things apart from money are important, such as parental interest in the child's progress, intellectual companionship, and other non-material factors. True, but on this argument high parental intelligence and above-average material possessions would have to produce a very strong negative set of IQ determinants. For consider: parents having an IQ of 140 have on the average come from a social background materially and intellectually inferior to that they themselves provide for their children. This can be inferred from the fact that some 30% of them would have been upwardly mobile socially. Yet their children have a mean IQ something like 20 points lower than their parents, although provided with all the advantages which we are told in other contexts constitute the environmental determinants of IQ! If, then, the immaterial environmental determinants mentioned above are much more frequently found in dull and socially improverished parents—and are so important that their absence in the affluent families produces a drop of 20 points of IQ in their children, and their presumed presence in the dullest, unskilled group produces a rise of 7 points of IQ in their children—why is it that middle-class children (and parents) are so significantly superior in IQ to working-class children (and parents)? This class difference is usually "explained" interms of precisely those material and intellectual advantages which characterise our higher professional parents. In other words, the environmentalist critics again want to have it both ways—factors are alleged to be important in relation to one set of facts, unimportant (or even negative in their effects) in relation to another. Such reasoning is clearly illogical. The facts are not compatible with any environmentalist hypothesis yet proposed, but are exactly as demanded by a theory combining hereditary with environmentalist determinants in the proportion of 4 to 1.

ONE FURTHER ARGUMENT deserves at least some mention. Cattell has suggested, as have several other writers, that the well-known fact that fertility is negatively correlated with IQ should result in a "dysgenic" trend in the national level of intelligence. In other words, if the dull have more children than the bright, then the dull will inherit the earth—or at least, their progeny will lower the national average IQ. Several studies have failed to show the predicted decline, but there are various reasons why this failure of the prediction is not fatal to the genetic hypothesis. In the first place, the studies showing a negative correlation between fertility and IQ were carried out on couples having at least one child. Usually the study began by locating children in school, and then ascertaining their IQ and the number of their siblings. But this leaves out of account both those who never marry (which includes an unduly high proportion of people with very low IQ's) and those who, though married, have no children. The data are therefore not of a kind to make possible any confident prediction. Far more would need to be known about the whole population and its reproductive history before we could venture to say what sort of change could be expected. In the second place, the genetic hypothesis does *not* say that environmental factors play *no part at all* in determining IQ scores. The 20% allocated to these factors allows of a considerable effect over the years, which could easily outweigh any dysgenic selection effects. In the third place, to test the hypothesis fairly would mean equating the groups tested for test sophistication and other factors known to influence IQ scores. This was quite clearly not done in the studies so far reported. It is not impossible, and would be very interesting, to study the variations (if any) in national IQ over the years. For the reasons given above I am unable to agree that the findings we have so far throw much light on the controversy.

THERE ARE CERTAIN QUALIFICATIONS which attach to every scientific statement, and these need to be explicitly stated in order to avoid confusion. I have already stated two of these. Estimates of heritability apply only to clearly marked populations, such as white citizens of England, and they apply only at a given moment of time, such as the decades from 1930 to 1960. Most importantly, the estimate does not necessarily apply to colored residents, either in the

U.S.A. or in the UK; special studies would be required to find out whether it does and these studies have not been made. This point should be borne in mind when considering the evidence about Negro IQ's to be discussed in the next chapter; it will be referred to again. It is not implied, of course, that the heritability estimate of U.S. Negroes would be necessarily different from the figure quoted; it seems likely that it would not differ very greatly from the 80% or so quoted for white populations. But we do not know, and we have no right to assume what has not been proven.

Another qualification, not often mentioned, is that the figure of 80% heritability is an average. It does not apply equally to every person in the country. For some people environment may play a much bigger part than is suggested by this figure; for others it may be even less. This misunderstanding may be responsible for the inability of psychiatrists, penologists and remedial educationalists to accept the figure. Professionally, they see very largely children and adults in whom environmental causes have been extremely influential in producing distortions of genetic potential, and a figure of 80% heritability does not seem reasonable to them. Nor is it—for this particular, very exceptional sample! The fact that the average height of Englishmen is 5 foot 10 inches does not mean that there are no giants or dwarfs. An average is an average is an average; it has certain advantages and certain disadvantages, and should not be misinterpreted or misunderstood.

Of particular interest to many critics of the heritabilty concept of the IQ is the phenomenon of early deprivation. Animal studies seem to suggest that severe deprivation of sensory input, or of motor movement, may have long-lasting and very debilitating effects on problem-solving abilities; and it is often suggested that these studies are relevant to the school experiences of "deprived" children. It should be noted that what we term "deprived" children are not in fact children treated anything like as severely as are the animals in these studies. Our "deprived" children correspond more to the non-deprived animals forming the control groups in these studies. When quite exceptionally socially isolated human children are taken out of their deprived environment into good, average social environments, they are found to make rapid increases in IQ and end up as average citizens, such children having a mean IQ of 105. Consider, as a particular example, Isabel. She was confined and reared in an attic up to the age of six by a deaf-mute mother. Her IQ was 30. When she was put into an average environment her IQ became normal by the age of 8, and she performed as an average student throughout school. Extreme environmental deprivation, thus, need not result in a permanent lowering of IQ below normal. In monkeys, too, extreme sensory deprivation and social isolation affect social behavior rather than ability for complex discrimination learning, delayed response learning, or the learning of set formation.

It is noteworthy that severely deprived children do not, in fact, behave anything like culturally disadvantaged children. When deprived children are restored to normal environments, their IQs rise quickly and permanently. Disadvantaged children show no such rapid rise, and the slight rises they do show are not permanent and they soon revert to their original levels. The whole literature on severe deprivation in animals is interesting psychologically, and important theoretically; but it is largely irrelevant to the heritability of IQ, even if such deprivation were more common than it fortunately is.

ANOTHER POINT, however, is relevant, and forms the basis of criticisms of the whole conception of heritability which are frequently heard. This is that our calculations disregard the importance of interaction between environment and heredity. Thus, intelligent children may select a different environment to grow up in than do dull children; this different environment in turn increases the difference in IQ. Michael Faraday was the son of a tinker and without much formal education, but he selected an environment which would sharpen his wits by attending the lectures given by Humphry Davy; he attracted his mentor's attention, and finally became his assistant and successor. George Washington Carver, the noted Negro biologist, was not allowed to attend school (which was reserved for white children) so he sat outside and acquired his education in this somewhat unorthodox manner. We select from many possible environments one that suits our genetic constitution. However, as long as these different environments are freely available, there is little evidence that this interaction complicates our mathematics unduly; its effect is relatively small and may for all practical purposes be disregarded. In other cultures this may not be true, of course, and in particular it may not be true of white-black comparisons.

Nevertheless, and in spite of the fact that modern genetic computations do take this factor into account, a brief discussion of some of the complexities which it gives rise to may be appropriate, because it may make it easier to follow our discussion of the origins of the black-white differences in IQ. It is most useful to start out with the distinction made by geneticists between *genotype* and *phenotype*. The former refers to the totality of factors that make up the genetic complement of an individual, while the latter refers to the totality of physically or chemically observable characteristics of an individual that results from the interaction of his genotype with his environment.* Different genotypes may give rise to the same phenotype (in different environments) and different phenotypes may be shown by the same genotypes.

This complexity is well shown by some often-quoted examples. Himalayan rabbits reared under ordinary conditions have a white body with black feet. When reared in a

*Environment is here more widely defined than is perhaps usual, and includes not only intra-uterine and post-natal conditions but also a variety of molecular factors acting within and between the embryonic cells.

warm cage, they do not show any evidence of black color, although genetically identical (same genotype, different environment).

Even more interesting and relevant is another study which investigated the interaction of heredity and environment in four breeds of dogs. Half of each litter was reared under "indulgent" conditions, the other half under "disciplined" conditions. (The litters were genetically pure, *i.e.* of practically identical heredity.) At eight weeks of age, the puppies were tested in a situation where the person who had reared them conditioned them not to eat, by swatting them over the rump whenever they approached the food dish. The effectiveness of the conditioning was then tested by the trainer leaving the room and observing the behavior of the puppies. Basenjis, who are natural psychopaths, ate as soon as the trainer had left, regardless of whether they had been brought up in the disciplined or the indulgent manner. Both groups of Shetland sheep dogs, loyal and true to death, refused the food, over the whole period of testing, *i.e.* eight days! Beagles and fox terriers responded differentially, according to the way they had been brought up; indulged animals were more easily conditioned, and refrained longer from eating. Thus, conditioning has no effect on one group, regardless of upbringing—has a strong effect on another group, regardless of upbringing—and affects two groups differentially, depending on their upbringing. Clearly interactions can be complex and difficult to disentangle, although in humans there is little likelihood of finding such marked differences in different racial strains as in these highly inbred litters of dogs.

A final experimental illustration which is directly relevant to our main theme is provided by a study by Cooper and Zubeck, who took two strains of maze-bright and maze-dull rats, bred for this characteristic over thirteen generations. Members of each group were reared in either a normal laboratory-rat environment, or in an enriched environment (in which slides, tunnels, balls, bells and other objects were provided, as well as complex visual stimuli), or in an impoverished environment (only food box and water pan being provided.) At sixty-five days of age the rats were tested on the Hebb-Williams maze, and their errors in running this maze counted (which is a reasonable intelligence test for rats). Findings were as follows. The enriched environment produced a considerable improvement over the natural habitat performance in the dull, but not the bright rats. Conversely, a restricted environment pushed up the error score of the bright rats, but left the dull ones unaffected. Note this interaction effect; but note also that, in contra-distinction to human conditions, the rats were assigned to conditions; they had no chance to select their preferred environment. This is an important difference.

BEFORE CLOSING this discussion of the nature of intelligence, and the measurement of IQ, we must consider an argument that is quite frequently presented by critics who wish to deny the possibility of genetic differences in racial comparisons. What they suggest, in essence, is that IQ as we measure it is defined by white psychologists, and that naturally black (and other colored) children and adults do less well on these tests than the whites for whom they were designed. The suggestion has been officially made by a group of black psychologists that a set of tests should be specially developed for blacks, on which, so it is suggested, whites would turn out to be inferior. This whole argument has a specious appearance of reasonableness, but in actual fact it is entirely mistaken.

In the first place, note that it assumes what it is intended to deny, namely the existence of racial differences in intelligence between blacks and whites. According to this argument, not only are blacks and whites quantitatively different; we are now asked to believe that the differences between blacks and whites are qualitative, that is, the intelligence of the one group is different in nature to that of the other. There is no evidence for such a far-reaching suggestion, and it may confidently be predicted that any attempts to find such tests will end in failure. It is perhaps valid to draw attention to the fact that in spite of many arguments along these lines put forward over the years, no black psychologist has ever published any results even suggestive that such Negro-favoring tests could be produced.

It might appear that Jensen kimself, as we shall see, posits two different kinds of "intelligence"—associative and conceptual. Are these not qualitatively different? It would be more profitable to regard them as approximations of two of Thurston's "primary factors" of intelligence, those of rote memory and of reasoning. They are not qualitatively different kinds of intelligence, but parts or portions of the more general concept. And in any case Jensen is not suggesting that blacks show one kind, whites another; both types of intelligence are found in both groups.

In the second place, note that what is true of blacks should also be true of other colored groups. Thus, descendants of oriental immigrants in California should also be handicapped by tests which were made by whites. But not a bit of it. Orientals suffer, almost if not quite as much as Negroes, from racial prejudice, and their socio-economic position is distinctly lower than that of whites (although not quite as low as that of blacks). Nevertheless their performance on white IQ tests is if anything superior to that of whites of higher socio-economic status, suggesting that these white tests make out orientals to be slightly brighter than whites. Surely there must be something wrong with an argument which produces such unexpected and contrary results.

In the third place, the argument seems to suggest that the choice of tests is entirely arbitrary—as if white psychologists had taken tests which put them at an advantage to blacks, and rejected tests which did not. But this is quite untrue. The selection of tests, and test items, is very largely objective and based on the observed relations between tests and test items, and on the predictive value of such tests for educational and professional purposes. Furthermore, the choice of tests and items fits in reasonably well with theories of the nature of intelligence, and even with physiological indices, such as the evoked potential differences between test-bright and test-dull subjects. Such evidence as there is does not suggest that these correlations and predictive indices are any different for black groups. Test-bright blacks do better educationally and professionally than do test-dull blacks, very much in the same manner as do whites.*

The argument is sometimes extended to include the whole educational system, as well as professional training. It is suggested that these call for, and select on the basis of, qualities which favor the white man, as opposed to the black. This is very likely true, but it does not seem very relevant.

The underprivileged populations of the Earth seek to control nature, and to build industrially and commercially viable civilizations. They require the services of engineers and

*The very extensive work done in the U.S.A. on prediction of success at university on the basis of high school records and IQ tests has demonstrated conclusively that high school records are less valid predictors for black than for white candidates. IQ test scores predict with equal accuracy for both blacks and whites. This is what we would expect if the former were more "culture bound," the latter more "culture fair." In any case the figures give no support to those who believe "white" tests do not apply to blacks, or enable predictions about their success or failure in tasks requiring intelligence to be made.

Another way of looking at this problem is to study in detail the psychometric properties of test-items for blacks and whites. Careful examinations of this kind have shown no consistent differences. Comparing difficulty levels of different items gives almost identical results for random samples of the two races.

On all the statistical comparisons made hitherto and reported in the literature, blacks and whites behave like two random samples from the same population. This is not compatible with the belief that the properties of IQ tests are changed when different racial populations growing up within the same culture are being measured.

What Is Intelligence?

scientists, lawyers and doctors, administrators and politicians, as well as skilled workers and able businessmen. Such persons need the kind of mental ability valued in our society, just as much as do similar people in white countries. Similarly, Negroes in the U.S.A. seek the rewards of our type of civilization—cars and refrigerators, television sets and vacuum cleaners, pleasant houses and good education. But these are the results of applying intelligence to the evolution of a political framework which allows industry and commerce to play their part, and to the creation of a body of scientific knowledge and engineering skill which can be translated into tangible rewards.

It is, of course, open to anyone to reject our type of civilization. But success, as measured in these terms, demands precisely the intellectual qualities measured by intelligence tests. It is unreasonable to reject the qualities and demand the fruits to which their application gives rise. Negroes demand access to schools and universities, and rightly so; but these are valued precisely because of their high standards of intellectual ability. It makes no sense to reject the very notion of such abilities as being important, and to advocate a theory of their being peculiar to the white race, and at the same time demand access to institutions closely geared to the view that such abilities are absolutely fundamental to successful study.

If training in universities and colleges is valued, either as important in itself or as leading to useful qualifications in medicine, or law, or some other profession, then the corollary must also be accepted, namely that "white man's IQ tests" are relevant to success in these studies. It is logically acceptable to reject white culture, white science, white civilization, white medicine and white IQ tests. It makes no sense to reject the last-named, but seek to acquire the former. What has been found requisite in creating and handing on the former has been precisely the ability imperfectly measured by IQ tests. Any lowering of standards of admittance with respect to IQ would demonstrably lead to a disastrous lowering of standards of competence in these fields among those graduating.

We must conclude that just as there is not one physics for Aryans, and another for Jews, so there is not one intelligence for whites, another quite different type for blacks. The ability to reason, to abstract, to educe relations and correlates, is fundamental to intelligent activity, to educational progress and to professional competence. The color of a man's skin has nothing to do with the truth or otherwise of these statements. IQ tests, imperfect as they undoubtedly still are, are a first step towards a better understanding, and a proper measurement, of these important aspects of human nature.

THERE IS ONE FURTHER POINT which needs to be discussed. It is often suggested that IQ tests may involve a self-fulfilling prophecy. Children testing low will be regarded by their teachers as likely to do poorly in their educational work, and this attitude will communicate itself to the children, discourage them, and lead to the very thing predicted—they will in fact do worse than they would otherwise have done. The work of Robert Rosenthal (particularly the book *Pygmalion in the Classroom* which he published with L. Jacobson) is often cited in this connection, and the impression is given that this is not an hypothesis, but an established fact. This is not so. There may be some truth in the hypothesis, but the evidence available to date is not such as to provide much evidence in its favor. Rosenthal's book has been severely criticized for obvious experimental and statistical errors, and it would be entirely premature to accept his evidence as conclusive. We do not, as of this writing, know if such an effect exists at all, or what it might amount to quantitatively; the hypothesis is an interesting one, and research into it is certainly to be encouraged. However, even the discovery of a correlation such as that postulated would not tell us anything about the causal sequences involved. Correlations do not tell us anything about causation, as elementary textbooks of statistics keep warning us, without much effect. Even if an effect could be demonstrated in due course, we would need to know something about the factors responsible for it before being able to estimate its influences on the determination of educational success by IQ. There are many theoretical possibilities, and in the absence of any ascertained facts little can be said with assurance.

BEFORE CONCLUDING this chapter, I would like to say a few words about the underlying fallacy of so many of the arguments which are presented by confirmed environmentalists in support of their cause.

It is a well-known axiom that correlation does not prove causation. In other words, two types of events may be correlated (*i.e.* found in conjunction) without one necessarily being the cause of the other. Thus, there is a very high correlation over the first seventy years of this century between the number of iron ingots shipped from Pennsylvania to California, and the number of registered prostitutes in Buenos Aires. This does not mean that either event or series of events caused the other in any meaningful manner. Similarly, the alleged fact that criminality is correlated with broken homes (there is some not very good evidence that criminals come from broken homes with greater frequency than do non-criminals matched for social class, education, etc.) does not prove that broken homes cause criminality, although environmentalists have drawn this conclusion for many years. It is possible that the personality traits which cause the home to be broken in the first place are heritable, and produce in the children the kind of behaviour we call criminal. The relation may be due to heredity, not to environmental factors at all. It is even possible that the presence in the family of a very difficult and even criminal child causes the break-up of the home, thus reversing the alleged causal chain! Many alternative possibilities suggest themselves, and without additional proof the evidence cannot be used to support the environmentalist hypothesis (or, of course, the genetic hypothesis). The interesting point, however, is that modern sociology is built almost entirely on arguments of precisely this nature. Environmentalist hypotheses exclusively are considered, and conclusions are based on evidence which is entirely correlational, and hence incapable of bearing this causal interpretation. Genetic arguments are not refuted by appeal to factual evidence; they are never even considered. Yet in most cases such genetic arguments have at least as much *a priori* force as the environmentalist arguments, and frequently there is strong evidence pointing their way. What is needed, clearly, is a methodology which is capable of unraveling this tangled skein.

A GOOD EXAMPLE of how such a methodology can be worked out, and how it may serve to shed unexpected light on an old controversy, can be found in the literature on cigarette smoking and its effects on health. Many empirical studies have found a strong correlation between smoking and various diseases, notably cardiovascular and respiratory. Official reports from respected bodies like Britain's Royal College of Physicians have argued that this correlation spells causation, and that the studies quoted demonstrate that smoking causes these diseases. In *Smoking, Health and Personality* (1965), I pointed out that the evidence was equally compatible with a hereditary model, and quoted evidence to show that personality factors, themselves known to be largely hereditary, were associated both with the development of such diseases as lung cancer, and with cigarette smoking. It seemed possible that heredity might predispose some people both to smoking and to diseases. The evidence, therefore, was ambiguous, and could not be interpreted with the confidence shown by the College of

Physicians. What was needed was not more of the same kind of old-fashioned research which in the nature of things could not bring forward proper proof of a causal type, but research taking into account the genetic hypothesis. Such research has now been done, and we know a good deal more than we did before. Cederlof, Lundman, Friberg, and their associates have studied tens of thousands of identical twins, one of whom was a smoker the other a non-smoker. In these comparisons heredity has been held constant (because in each pair of identical twins there are no differences in heredity, both having inherited the same set of genes) so that any differences found would be due to smoking. What was the outcome? No differences between smokers and non-smokers were found for cardiovascular diseases (such as coronary heart disease); thus by eliminating genetic factors, the correlation between smoking and cardiovascular disease was also eliminated! For respiratory diseases the conclusion was quite different. Here, differences between smokers and non-smokers remained, even in the twin sample, proving that this correlation was indeed associated with a direct causal connection.

Here, then, we have an example of a study in which both the genetic and the environmentalistic hypotheses were properly tested, and where preconceived notions were not allowed to determine the design or the conclusions. The result is that we now know something about the consequences of cigarette smoking where previously we were reduced to guessing. Sociology, on the whole, has not learned the lesson of science: that knowledge cannot be acquired by leaving out of account alternative hypotheses, and concentrating on those which appeal to the research worker's prejudices. Genetic causes may not be palatable to those who would change the shape of the world; but this is not good or sufficient reason for failing to consider them in one's research paradigms.

4
THE INTELLIGENCE OF
AMERICAN NEGROES

WE HAVE ALREADY noted that the difficulties in comparing intelligence between groups differing not only in race but also in general cultural background, (e.g. American whites and African Negroes) are such that at the moment only exploratory research is possible. There are certain interesting findings which are somewhat peripheral, although certainly not irrelevant. It is repeatedly reported that African Negro children (and American Negro children as well) show highly precocious sensori-motor development, as compared with white norms. Thus, most of the African Negro babies who were drawn up to a sitting position could keep head erect and back straight from the very first day of life; white babies typically require six to eight weeks to sustain these postures! It is implausible to assert that socio-economic differences or other extrinsic variables (particularly in so far as these disfavor Negroes) could have produced this astonishing difference. The observed precocity lasts for about three years, after which time white children overtake the black ones. These findings are important because of a very general law in biology according to which the more prolonged the infancy, the greater in general are the cognitive or intellectual abilities of the species. This law appears to work even within a given species. Sensori-motor precocity in humans, as shown in so-called "baby-tests" of intelligence, is negatively correlated with terminal IQ.

This early advantage in sensori-motor coordination is not preserved by Negroes. There is much evidence to show that at later ages they are on the average inferior to whites on many diverse tests involving this ability and other related ones. One or two examples, taken from the work of Noble, must suffice to illustrate this phenomenon. Figure 8 shows the performance on the pursuit rotor of white and black children, using the right hand and also the left hand. (In this test the children have to follow the movement of a metal disc superimposed on a round, rotating gramophone turn-table with a metal stylus; the score is the length of time they manage to keep the stylus on target, *i.e.* in contact with the metal disc.) The results show a very marked difference for the right hand, and a very small difference for the left, which is of course much less capable than the right; even so, the Negroes do less well with the right than the whites with the left. The test is of interest because it does not involve any appreciable verbal or cognitive ability, and has been shown to involve very strong hereditary determination of success. Figure 9 shows a similar comparison for discrimination reaction time, *i.e.* the speed with which the children can react to diverse stimuli. It will be seen that to begin with there is little difference; but as the test continues, and learning begins to play a part, the whites shoot ahead. These results are fairly typical of many others in this field. Note that it would be difficult to account for the results in terms of motivational factors, or in terms of long-continued discrimination. If these factors were important, then why are the races so poorly distinguished on the pursuit rotor when the left hand is used, and why are there no differences at the beginning of the reaction time task? We shall return to these environmental hypotheses for inferior Negro performance later.

Early precocity of Negro children, and later falling away, has also been observed by Bayley in her large-scale studies of children and their perceptual-motor development. Interestingly enough, several observers have found Japanese and

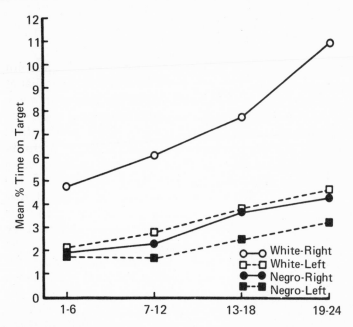

8 Differences in pursuit rotor performance, with right and left hand respectively, of white and Negro subjects. The graph shows the average time on target achieved by each sample in successive blocks of twenty ten-second trials.

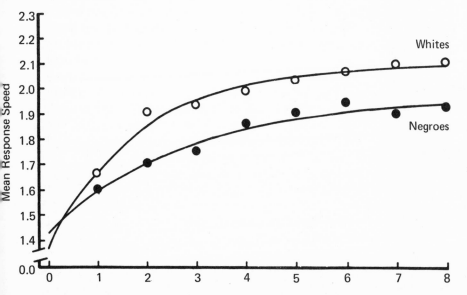

9 Mean speed of response of white and Negro children in discrimination reaction time experiments. The speeds are shown for successive twenty-trial blocks.

Chinese infants to be less precocious on such tests than Caucasian ones. At higher ages, oriental children do significantly better than white ones on such typical perceptual-motor tests as the "figure copying task"; Negro children do worse. This superiority of oriental over white children is surprising when it is considered that their socio-economic status is well below that of the whites. Taken together with the superiority of oriental adults on tests of abstract reasoning (in spite of the same inferiority in socio-economic status) one might conclude that orientals may have genetically superior gene-pools for doing IQ tests manufactured by whites!

Whatever may be the explanation of the oriental superiority in face of socio-economic inferiority, it poses a problem for environmentalist explanations. How can we account for the fact that oriental children coming from homes of low socio-economic status perform as well as, or better than do white children coming from homes of middle-class status on tests of abstract reasoning? A similar problem is posed by the fact that, as we shall see, the opposite is true of Negroes. Whites of low socio-economic status score better on IQ tests than do blacks of high status. Consideration of these points must be deferred until we have had a chance to discuss the evidence.

WHEN WE TURN to the direct measurement of intelligence, we are almost entirely restricted to work with American Negroes. Only there do we have a sufficiently uniform background to make comparisons between blacks and whites fruitful. This proposition is, of course, hotly contested by environmentalists who declare that we are dealing here with a sub-culture so different from the major (white) culture that no realistic and meaningful comparisons can in fact be made. Fortunately this objection is subject to empirical investigation, in so far as it issues in specific objections which can be assigned some factual content; many such investigations have been carried out, and will be reported presently. To be sure, it is essential for critics to make their objections in as precise a manner as possible. Vague and nebulous statements are inherently untestable, and therefore cannot be refuted. Critics have a duty, much the same as the proponents of a proposition, to be as factual as possible and to make assertions which are testable. Just as theories which are not falsifiable are not taken seriously by scientists, so criticisms which are not falsifiable are not taken seriously either. It is always possible to appeal to unspecified agencies, mysterious and all-embracing, which might have produced the observed results; but to do so is not very useful in the scientific study of observed events.

In surveying the results of work in this field, I have done little but paraphrase the scholarly, extensive and very reliable summary published by Audrey M. Shuey, entitled *The Testing of Negro Intelligence* (2nd edition 1966). Anyone interested in the field will find there, on almost 600 pages, detailed and often tabulated research data from almost 400 separate empirical investigations. It would clearly be impossible to go into similar detail here, as well as being supererogatory—such a job needed to be done, but having been well done, requires no repetition. Readers who wish to consult the references on which my own summaries and conclusions are based can do no better than read Shuey. Although I am familiar with most of this literature I have not been able to fault the book on any factual statement, and neither have other professional critics. The facts are all there, and they are not really in dispute. As regards their interpretation, we will have to discuss that later on.

SHUEY BEGINS by surveying a number of studies of young pre-school children, between the ages of two and six. These are mostly enrolled in nurseries, day nurseries, kindergarten or summer school, and are hardly likely to be random samples of the population. Several conclusions appear to be supported by the data. On the average, the IQ of the colored children is 12 points below that of the white children of the same age. But this difference is decreased—not eliminated—when white children are chosen on the basis of living in the same neighborhood, attending the same school, and having fathers in the same occupational group as the black children. The disparity between the races has increased rather than decreased in the last twenty years or so, in spite of a greater proportional improvement in the educational facilities for Negroes.

School children have been tested in much larger numbers than pre-school children, and being a captive group sampling is much more representative. Data are based on some 80,000 Negro children in all. Negro children come out with an IQ of 84; this mean is not affected by mode of testing (individual or group; verbal or non-verbal tests). Southern colored children have a mean IQ of 80, Northern of 88. There is no tendency, as has sometimes been suggested, for the IQ of Negro children to decline as they get older and progress through school. "Between the ages of seven and twelve and between grades one and seven there is a marked stability in the IQ of colored children enrolled in the public schools." It is possible to restrict comparisons between white and black children to cases where these come from the same or similar neighborhoods and have parents of matched socio-economic status. When this is done the difference between white and black children is reduced to between 8 and 13 points, with an approximate mean difference of 11 points, rather than the overall difference of 15 points. Shuey argues that "the size of this remaining difference does not warrant our assuming that racial differences in IQ would be eradicated with further steps towards equality of opportunity" . . . The argument appears to be that if equalizing the grossest and most obvious socio-economic differences, including educational ones, only produces a decline in the difference between white and black children from 15 points to 11 points, then it is unlikely that the comparatively slight remaining differences, if they could be successfully eradicated, would account for all of the remaining 11 points. It is sometimes suggested that Negro children are less highly motivated, or respond to different motivations. This is not borne out by such research (admittedly inadequate) as has been reported. Money and candy rewards only led to small improvements in the performance of Negro children, and in their pattern of reaction to different types of incentive they did not notably differ from white children.

High-school students in the U.S.A. correspond somewhat to children in secondary education, comprehensive or grammar, in Britain. The mean IQ's of black and white children in these schools do not differ very much from the means reported from primary school children; for Southern children of Negro origin the mean IQ is 82, for Northern children of Negro origin it is 91. Two findings stand out as of some interest. In the first place, several investigations were conducted with black testers administering the IQ tests: "there seems to be no evidence that the race of the examiner materially affected the testing rapport. ..." It has often been suggested that black children naturally react poorly when tested by white examiners or teachers; they appear to do no better when tested by examiners or teachers of their own color. The other finding relates to the pattern of differences between black and white when different types of mental tests are examined. It is found that contrary to what one might have expected on the environmentalist hypothesis, Negro children are more inferior on non-cultural (culture fair) than on cultural items, and on non-language than on language ones. When black and white children were matched on a verbal test, the black children were found to be inferior on a performance test. Environmentalists would have predicted (and have, in fact, predicted) exactly the opposite. We shall return to this point again.

There is much misunderstanding in Britain, but also in the U.S.A., about the actual quality of the education offered to

Negro children, as compared with white children. The official Coleman report, which surveyed 645,000 pupils in more than 3,000 schools in all regions of the United States, found relatively minor differences in the measured characteristics of schools attended by different racial and ethnic groups. Jensen correlated published statistics for 191 school districts in the ten counties of the Greater Bay area in California and found that "minority enrolment has quite negligible correlations with all the school facility variables except number of administrators per hundred pupils, and this correlation is positive." In other words, the proportion of Negro children in a given district is not at all related to such factors as "per pupil expenditure," "teacher-pupil ratio," or "teacher salary." This finding should not be generalized over the whole country; nor would it have been true fifty years ago, when Negro children undoubtedly suffered from a gross lack of facilities. Nevertheless, IQ differences between whites and blacks are as large as ever in spite of the equalization of educational facilities. Nor does it appear that desegregation— which is of course desirable on other grounds—has had any effect on the scholastic achievement of Negro children. Alan B. Wilson found that after controlling for other factors, the racial composition of the school had no significant direct association with Negro achievement. A similar conclusion was reached by S. Bowles and H.M. Kevin, in their analysis of the figures published in the Coleman report. These figures challenge widely-held beliefs about increasing the effectiveness of education by commonsense improvements in size of class, remuneration of teachers, and money spent. Even so, the conclusion of the Coleman report "that schools bring little influence to bear on a child's achievement that is independent of his background and general social context" is probably exaggerated and can be faulted by a proper statistical re-analysis of their data. Further research into these almost axiomatic beliefs would surely seem to be in order.

One such research project is of particular interest. Called

"Project Learn Well," it was instituted at Raphael Weill School in San Francisco in an attempt to go all out to improve the scholastic achievement of disadvantaged children (mostly Negroes) by having such a small pupil/teacher ratio as to permit private tutoring of each child. When the actual advances these children made were compared with state-wide norms, it was found that if anything they had actually fallen even further behind, and the program was appraised as "a complete and utter failure."

Community and school leaders, while admitting that the children had fallen behind in school achievement, claimed that other goals of the program were being met. It was said that the children's self-image was improved, and that the community was more closely involved in school affairs. This may be so, and such consequences would of course be desirable. Yet the hard fact remains that the program was instituted to bring the children up to scratch educationally, and instead made them worse. This is not an isolated instance of such attempts, and such failures, to come to grip with the educational problems presented by disadvantaged children (black and white). When will educationalists learn that good will and good intentions are not enough to produce favorable results, in the absence of scientific knowledge about the best ways of going about this business? Readers may like to consider what kind of outcome they would have expected from such apparently desirable improvements in the general management of a school, and to contrast this with the miserable results actually achieved. They might also like to extrapolate the differences between hope and achievement to Britain and consider that there too proposals for improvements are based entirely on unverified assumptions and commonsense premises which might not stand up to empirical test. This is not to suggest that all is for the best in the best of all possible worlds, and that no changes are needed. The suggestion is rather that ignorance is a bad teacher, and that research should precede application.

WHEN WE COMPARE college students, as being one rung higher on the educational ladder, we again encounter problems of representativeness and selection. Both white and black university students are highly selected, and one might expect this process of selection to reduce the difference. This does not seem to be so. When comparisons are made, only 10% of white students score below the average of the black students, and 90% score above. Shuey comments: "It is evident that Negro college students, on the average, have earned lower scores on mental or scholastic aptitude tests than have white students. It is also evident, judged from comparisons of average scores, mean percentile ranks, and amounts of overlapping, that they do not approach the white norms as closely as do Negro children, in spite of the fact that Negro college students probably represent a relatively highly selected sampling of their racial group." (It can be shown, in fact, that Negro students are even more selected than are white students, in the sense of constituting a smaller proportion of their total group.)

Shuey deals with the assumption made by many people that the poorer showing of Negroes at the college level rests upon cumulative effects of early poor schooling of many Negro college students and the probably cumulative effect of a more restricted, less complex environment, and the sub-standard situations to which these students have been subjected during their lives. "However, the following points —namely (1) the low scoring of colored students in institutions of higher learning for Negroes, (2) the inferior showing of Negroes attending mixed northern universities as compared with whites in the same universities, (3) the unfavorable averages of coloreds coming south to college from mixed northern secondary schools as compared with the norms, (4) the evidence that greater inter-racial differences occur in the more highly abstract tests than in those dealing with concrete or practical problems, and (5) the greater selectivity of the Negro as compared with the white college student—cast serious doubt upon the assumption that the obtained differences are completely or primarily due to inferior patterns of speech and to the cumulative effect of an inferior environment." These points are of course suggestive, not conclusive. As I have pointed out several times, we must not look for crucial experiments, but rather for mutual support among different lines of proof and argument.

One very carefully chosen sample of white and black men was studied in order to see whether equating them on a large variety of background data, personality measures, and test-taking attitude would eliminate the observed differences. Matching was done on age, education, occupation of parents, income of parents, geographical area of childhood home, army rank, number of years in service, marital status, urban or rural background, and plans for re-enlistment, as well as on the personality and test-taking variables. Very significant differences of 10 to 14 points were again found, in spite of these efforts to eliminate socio-economic differences and "intellectually defeating personality traits" from the comparison. The relevance of such attempts to equate for background factors will be discussed later on; let us note merely that while there is some reduction in the difference between blacks and whites, this reduction is not very marked.

WE MUST NOW TURN to studies made of special groups of whites and blacks, and the first to be discussed are the gifted (arbitrarily defined, following Terman in his *Studies of Genius*, as having an IQ of 140 or above) and the retarded. Results of many studies are fairly well in agreement. "From a combination of relatively unselected samples of white and colored school children, it appears that proportionally the colored gifted have been reported about one sixth as often as the white gifted and that the colored retarded have been reported about six times as often as the white retarded." Some such proportion might have been expected from the general distribution of IQ's, and the mean differences between whites and blacks. Nevertheless, these figures are useful because they do not depend on extrapolations from curves which may not be strictly applicable to extreme groups (*i.e.* the gifted and the retarded).

These figures require some comment and indeed qualification in view of rather odd sex differences among blacks which only exist in an embryonic form among whites. It is universally found that, among Negroes, girls and women do better on IQ tests than do boys and men. Jensen has calculated that the difference is about 3 to 4 points of IQ in favor of the females. This is, of course, minute, but assumes considerable importance when we consider selection procedures (as for university education, or high-level jobs) which operate at the extreme end of the distribution of IQ's. Consider Figure 10, which shows in diagrammatic form the distribution of whites, and of male and female blacks, with

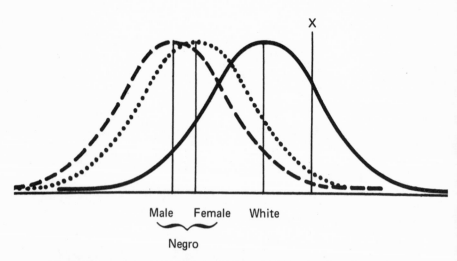

10 Diagrammatic distribution of IQ's of whites, black males and black females. X marks some arbitrary minimum ability point on the IQ scale for college admission or similar qualifications.

The IQ Argument

respect to intelligence test scores. The line drawn at X is meant to indicate the level at which selection for some forms of high-level job or education operates. It will be seen that at this extreme end of the distribution females constitute over twice as large a number of acceptable choices as do males, and both are of course exceeded by the whites. This is the kind of selection problem with which colleges and industries are faced. What does in fact happen? The Moynihan report has shown that among blacks the disparity in educational attainment of male and female youths aged sixteen to twenty-one is striking. Among the non-white males, 34% were high school graduates, compared with 45% of the females. A similar difference existed at the college level, with 4.5% of the non-white males having completed one to three years of college compared with 7.3% of the females. Examination of the honor rolls in Negro schools disclosed that 75 to 90% of all Negro honor students are girls. Among finalists for the Ford Foundation's National Achievement Scholarship Program for outstanding Negro high school graduates, 57% were girls. In a comparable National Merit Scholarship Program for whites, 67% of the award winners were boys. The causes of this difference in IQ are not known, nor is it known why the difference is larger in blacks than in whites. Whatever the explanation, the facts suggest that Negro males are even farther below white mean scores than is indicated by the figures quoted in this chapter, while Negro females are less far below whites in IQ. These facts are of course likely to exacerbate the problems which society has to face in relation to the generally low Negro IQ scores.

Delinquents and criminals constitute another special sample. Here, too, differences between whites and blacks continue to be significant, with a mean IQ for the whites of 92 and for the blacks of 81. When colored criminals were matched with white criminals for occupation, school grade completed, and type of community from which they had come, the differences between the means continued to be significant, although somewhat reduced.

HAVING SURVEYED the scores of children and students, we now turn to adults. Much the most widespread testing in that field has of course taken place in connection with army induction and selection procedures, and the role played by results reported from the 1916-1918 testing has already been mentioned. The general conclusion arrived at from the examination of enlisted men then was that Negroes were about one standard deviation (equal to 15 points of IQ) below whites, and testing of whites and Negroes during and after the Second World War has not changed this conclusion. Scores between the two racial groups are as discrepant as ever.

In some ways this is curious—one might have expected the relatively greater improvement in school and other facilities for Negroes to have brought the two samples closer together. There are other reasons for expecting such a lessening of the gap to occur. These are all connected with the fact that more colored than white inductees were screened out prior to testing. "This was due, in large part, to the fact that only about three-fourths as many Negroes as whites in proportion to their number were accepted for induction into the Armed Forces, to the fact that the differential rejection rate is not explainable on the basis of relatively more physical disqualifications among the Negroes but to there being more unintelligent illiterates among them, to the fact that relatively fewer occupational deferments were given to Negroes because of special abilities or skills, to the fact that some advantage was given to Negro enlisted men in several comparisons, and to the fact that there was a much larger percentage of superior whites than superior Negroes who made up the commissioned officer group and were not included in the statistics for enlisted men." In other words, the Negro sample is favored because the lowest IQ scorers were rejected on the grounds of illiteracy before induction and testing, and because a much larger group of high IQ whites was removed from the white sample of enlisted men, and counted as officers instead. It should be noted that this superiority of whites over Negroes in IQ among enlisted men also "holds true in comparisons between the northern Negro and the southern white draft, although the differences between these groups is less marked than between the northern Negro and the northern white or between the southern Negro and the southern white."

Of particular interest to some investigators have been comparisons between groups of Negroes differing in skin color, *i.e.* groups where one would expect different degrees of white admixture. The reasons for this interest are of course not far to seek. If whites are superior to blacks in IQ genetically, then an admixture of white ancestry should produce off-spring with higher IQ's, on the average, than would be found in the offspring of pure black ancestry. The argument is not as strong as it sounds because skin color, although it can be measured with some degree of accuracy, is only one index of white ancestry, and does not correlate all that highly with serological and other indices. Investigators who take this argument seriously would be well advised to use several morphological and serological measures in their studies. Conversely, if differences are in fact found between groups differing in darkness of skin, it might be argued that the very fact that such differences could be discovered with an imperfect measure of white admixture suggests that much greater differences would be found with more perfect measures. This might be true, were it not for the fact that having a lighter skin makes Negroes more acceptable to whites, and also gives them greater status within the Negro community. In this way superior IQ might be acquired through accidents of environmental origin. A good study might be designed by ascertaining independently by serological and morphological means the degree of "whiteness" of large samples of Negroes. The correlation between the two sets of indices is sufficiently low to make it possible to single out groups different on the serological tests, but identical on the morphological ones. These Negroes would all look equally "negroid," but would have different degrees of white ancestry. Degree of white ancestry could then be correlated with IQ without having to bother about lighter skin color having procured environmental advantages to some. Conversely, groups could be constructed of similar serological status, but differing in morphological factors. Here we would be able to study the influence of adventitious external factors, due to acceptability on the grounds of looks, when admixture of white ancestry was kept equal. It is to such studies that one must look to solve some of the puzzles presented to us by the complex interaction present in our society between heredity and environment. (Somewhat similar studies have been suggested by W. Shockley, the Nobel Prize winner, and Professor L.L. Heston.)

However, in the absence of such studies we must make do with what we have. There are eighteen studies in which hybrids were studied with respect to IQ; and in twelve of these those lighter in color, or identified as of mixed blood, scored higher than the darker more negroid in features, or those identified as of unmixed blood. In four other studies, the former groups had the advantage in most but not all of the tests used, while in two studies there were no differences correlated with morphological indices. Lighter, mixed groups are therefore on the whole more likely to have higher IQ scores than darker, unmixed individuals, and while the differences are not large, they might be considerably larger if better measures had been chosen to index the amount of white ancestry. It is difficult to disprove the argument that Negroes of lighter skin color might have had certain advantages because of their particular morphological characteristics; but such advantages as have been detailed do not seem particularly relevant to success on IQ tests. What is certain is that the possibilities of this method of investigation have not yet been realized; it holds out considerable promise for the future.

THE PROMISE HAS ALREADY been redeemed to some extent in a recent study by Lemos which appeared after Shuey's book was published. This work deals with Australian aboriginal children, rather than with American Negroes. But similar arguments about the environmental or genetic basis of the inferiority on IQ tests of coloreds to whites have been current in respect to this group also, and the findings are quite relevant to our discussion. Lemos used as her test of intellectual ability the development of Dr. Jean Piaget's concept of "conservation." In his theory this marks the beginning of logical thinking and the transition from a pre-operational to an operational level of thought. He found an invariant order of development of the notion of conservation of quantity, weight, and volume, and Lemos showed similar invariance with aboriginal children. It cannot therefore be argued that the test was not applicable to them, or that they showed different stages of development to those found by Piaget. The relevance of these tests to IQ is, of course, the age at which the various stages are achieved; the higher the IQ, the earlier are the concepts of conservation reached.

The children tested were subdivided into full aboriginals and part-aboriginals, the latter having a small degree of European ancestry. The classification was based on the mission records, and the majority of part-aboriginals were only one part in eight of white ancestry, that is, they had one great-grandparent who was white. This is, of course, not sufficient to make any difference to their appearance, and this part-white ancestry was not known to the other children. There was no evidence of any difference in cultural or environmental treatment between the full and part aboriginals. "Part-aborigines and full aborigines formed a single integrated community, and the children were brought up under the same mission conditions and attended the same school." Thus this study avoids the main pitfalls of the American studies. Classification of children is not on the basis of fallible external morphological signs, but on the basis of precise records. There are no external differentials which might lead to one group of children being given differential environmental, educational, or occupational treatment. Finally, the children themselves are ignorant of the admixture of white blood in themselves, or in other children.

Under these conditions, it may come as a surprise that the part-aboriginal children did markedly better on all the tests, of which there were six: conservation of quantity, weight, volume, length, area, and number. The observed differences were not just statistically significant though relatively small. They were, in fact, quite surprisingly large and consistent. Lemos, after carefully looking for environmental causes of this difference, concludes that they "cannot be attributed to environmental factors." She speculates that "in the case of aborigines factors such as genetic drift, extreme environmental conditions and natural selection could have operated to produce differences in intellectual potential between aborigines and other groups. It would therefore seem reasonable to attribute the significant differences between the part and the full aborigines in this study to genetic differences between aborigines and Europeans, resulting in the part aboriginal children having a higher probability of inheriting a higher intellectual potential." In considering these results, it is important to remember that the white ancestry involved is in fact very small, constituting something like 15% at the most. The fact that such small differences can be picked out by this method suggests that it may have tremendous potential for future research.

It might be thought that perhaps the records in the mission might not be entirely accurate, and that this inaccuracy might be fatal to the conclusion. This is not so. In the first place the event being chronicled is sufficiently obvious, at the time, to leave little doubt about its occurrence. In the second place, any recording errors would mitigate against the hypothesis of genetic causality, and attenuate the final results, by misclassifying part-aborigines as full, or full aborigines as part-aborigines. On the whole, this study must stand as one of the many props for the genetic hypothesis which environmentalists will find difficult to dislodge.

ONE FURTHER SPECIAL GROUP which has been of some interest to investigators has been the migrant Negro, in particular the child born in the south but taken by his parents to the north and there tested in his new school. Negro children of this type typically average 3 to 4 points of IQ lower than northern-born Negro children attending the same schools. This is about half the difference of 7 points usually observed between southern and northern children of Negro parentage. This reduction of the difference may be due to one of two main factors, or to a combination of both. Early writers used to assume that it was due to selective migration—the brighter Negroes left the south and went to the north where they might hope to better themselves. This hypothesis would suggest that the observed higher scores of the migrant children, as compared with the stay-at-homes, were due to hereditary factors. Later writers prefer an environmental hypothesis. They suggest that the better schooling available in the north, and other similar environmental factors, are responsible for the rise in score of migrant children. Shuey examines the available evidence with great care, and comes to the conclusion that neither hypothesis is ruled out, but also that neither hypothesis accounts for all the facts. Both may be assumed to account for approximately half the observed effect— which of course is rather small in any case. It is doubtful if these investigations throw much light on the problem of genetic differences in IQ between blacks and whites. Much more could have been done by testing parents as well as children, or by testing children before as well as after migration. In the absence of such data no certain conclusions can be drawn from the facts. The studies in question would not in fact have been mentioned at all in this survey if they had not often been cited as proving one point of view or the other; it is unfortunate that they are irrelevant to any firm conclusion.

THERE ARE FACTS which throw doubts on the hypothesis that inferior schooling in the southern states is responsible for the observed IQ differences. The Coleman report found that southern Negro children scored higher on verbal and scholastic achievement tests, relative to the non-verbal intelligence test, which Negroes in the north and west scored lower on the verbal and scholastic tests relative to the non-verbal test. Negroes in the rural south showed the largest discrepancy between the non-verbal and achievement tests, with higher scores in the scholastic achievement tests. These data are exactly the opposite to what one would have expected on the "poor schools in the south" hypothesis. Compared to their IQ level, southern Negro children are in fact superior to northern Negro children on scholastic tests.

An issue which has often been raised by critics of the testing of Negro intelligence has been the problem of the race of the tester. It has been suggested that white testers may inspire feelings of terror, or inadequacy, or hatred in the children tested; or that they fail to produce maximum motivation in them. The possibility that such factors might be operative cannot, of course, be gainsaid. But in science the task of a constructive critic goes beyond suggesting possible sources of error; it becomes necessary to demonstrate that the alleged errors actually occur. Such attempts have been made several times, and attention has already been drawn to one such study in which the race of the tester proved to be immaterial. This has been pretty much the general finding, although slight and sometimes significant differences have been found by individual investigators in both directions. In other words, Negro children sometimes do slightly better with Negro than with white testers, and sometimes they do better with white than with Negro testers. There are some suggestions in the literature that this "race" effect may be confounded with such other factors as difficulty of task, or anxiety produced by calling the test an "intelligence" test rather than an "eye-hand coordination" test. Studies experimentally comparing the effects of white and black testers agree in finding only small and inconsistent differences. Shuey selected nineteen studies in which Negro elementary children had been tested by a Negro, and compared the mean IQ from these studies with comparable ones in which white testers had been employed. The respective means were 80.9 and 80.6. A similar study of high school children produced mean IQ's of 82.9 and 82.1. "From these comparisons it would seem that the intelligence scores of a Negro school child or high school pupil has not been adversely affected by the presence of a white tester."

Another possible reason for differences is motivation. It is often suggested that Negro children are not motivated to do well in IQ tests, that they expect to do badly and consequently do not exert themselves, that they have low levels of aspiration due to cultural factors and occupational discrimination, and that quite generally they do not do themselves justice on such tests. This, again, is an hypothesis which might very well be true; as it happens it does not seem to hold up very well in experimental study.

There are two lines of argument and experimentation which seem to suggest that motivation has unexpectedly little influence on success in IQ tests. The first line of evidence relates to studies in which white children and adults have been studied and compared under motivating and non-motivating conditions. This may be done either by testing two randomly selected groups, motivating one but not the other by suitable instructions, by promises of money, candy, or other desirable gifts if they manage to do well, or by impressing them with the consequences of doing well or badly (for example, being promoted to the next higher form in school). Or it may be done by testing a large group, then splitting it up and retesting one sub-group under motivating conditions, the other under non-motivating conditions. Studies of both kinds have found no increments in IQ due to motivation, or at most rather small ones. Usually these are less than would be due to simple familiarity with the test on retesting.

One of my early studies might serve as an example of what happens in such experiments. Members of the armed services were tested on arrival at the Mill Hill Emergency Hospital, before assignment to their respective wards. The men would be tired, worried, and in a very low state of motivation. They were retested at the time of their leaving the hospital, either under non-motivating conditions (the test was presented as a routine one) or under motivating conditions (they were promised half a week's pay in cigarettes if they beat their previous score by 10 points or more.) There could be no doubt, from the remarks and general behavior of the patients, that this was a definite incentive to do well. In the event, both groups improved. The incentive group improved on the average by 1.52 points, and the non-incentive group by 1.96 points! This result, showing no effect of motivation on IQ, is fairly typical, although sometimes small increments do appear. They never amount to much, however, and in general Spearman's dictum that "cognition is independent of conation" has been upheld by such research as has been published. This also extends to studies in which test-takers are asked to rate their own interest in the outcome, and the effort they have put into the test; correlations with success are universally low or insignificant.

The second line of investigation directly attacks the problem of Negro motivation by extending this work, which has been done on white children and adults, to Negroes. One or two such studies have already been mentioned; others are quoted by Shuey. They do not give results in any way different to those found in whites. Conditions clearly acting in a direction of increased motivation do not seem to have much effect on Negro children, any more than on white children. Nor has it been found that Negro children have in fact lower vocational and educational aspirations than whites; the few differences that have been found are if anything in the opposite direction. Thus, the picture painted by critics of the Negroes as poorly motivated, non-aspiring and consequently doing poorly is not in line with the experimental evidence. Negroes do aspire to better education, better jobs and higher-paid positions, just as whites do. And just like the whites, Negroes seem to be self-motivated to a degree that makes the additive effects of further, external motivation almost irrelevant to success on IQ tests. The evidence suggests that Negro children, just like white children, are trying to do well on these tests (which after all have their own attraction and motivating properties—otherwise why would several million people have paid money to buy copies of my Penguin books presenting them with typical IQ test items?) and that this factor of motivation is not a very relevant one to the question of the observed score discrepancies.

THE ARGUMENT is sometimes extended to the assumed lower self-esteem of the Negro. It is suggested that in an environment which consistently discriminates against him, and in which he can do nothing right, the Negro loses self-esteem, and that this may lead him to failure in IQ tests. Here too the evidence suggests that there is not much truth in the argument. Shuey reviews the published work on this topic, and concludes: "Basing our opinion on the results of the various studies noted above, we would conclude that at the pre-school level there seems to be some evidence of awareness of color differences and a feeling of inferiority associated with dark skin, but at the grade school level and continuing through high school and college, there is no consistent evidence of lower self-esteem in Negroes; if there is a difference, it would appear to be more likely that Negroes have a greater sense of personal worth, rather than the reverse."

A point not hitherto made by psychologists critical of the hereditarian point of view, but which may have greater validity than those mentioned so far, relates to possible personality differences between blacks and whites. Negroes tend to come out much more extroverted on suitable tests, whites as more introverted. This difference is related to that between black "soul" and white "up-tightness." Now one major characteristic of extroversion is a marked degree of impulsiveness, and indeed there is much in Negro behavior to suggest that impulsiveness is indeed more clearly apparent in them than in whites. But impulsiveness can easily lead a person to obtain lower IQ test marks than his ability would warrant. He may make silly errors which on consideration he would have been easily able to correct. There is experimental evidence that disadvantaged children benefit considerably from test-taking instructions under which they are prevented from returning an answer to a given problem for some twenty seconds. This enables them to evaluate possible solutions, rather than proceed on a simple trial-and-error basis. I am not familiar with tests of this kind being carried out on black and white groups of children, but it is possible that IQ differences might be diminished. General training in "control" might raise scores on a more permanent basis. This hypothesis would seem well worth investigating.

WE MUST NOW TURN to a more detailed consideration of a point already mentioned on one or two occasions, namely the comparison of black and white samples equated, as far as possible, on socio-economic status, education, and other similar variables. The logic of this approach has given rise to much rather confused argument, and it may be useful to disentangle the various strands, even though we have already looked at some of the evidence.

If we assume that environmental causes alone are responsible for the low IQ's observed in Negro samples, then we would expect that equating environment for whites and blacks would bring them close together, or even make them have identical IQ's. If such an effect were found, it could of course also be explained on genetic grounds, and the results would therefore not be very revealing with respect to the discussion about the relative importance of these different causes. However, the actual findings are entirely different, and consequently we need not worry about what might have been. The suggestion that it is "fairer" to keep socio-economic status constant in making racial comparisons is certainly not acceptable. If the races are innately different with respect to IQ, then more Negroes would drift into the lower strata of the working class, and more whites into the upper strata of the middle class. It would artificially lower the mean white IQ, and raise the mean black IQ, to equate for socio-economic status if that is in fact partially a consequence of IQ in the first place. Such comparisons are interesting scientifically, but have nothing to do with "fairness."

We have already noted that when educational and socio-economic differences between samples of blacks and whites compared for IQ are reduced or eliminated, marked score differences still remain. These differences appear to be much greater at the upper than at the lower end of the social scale. Averaging the results from several investigations, Shuey found that when both blacks and whites came from high status groups, the mean IQ difference was 20; when both came from low status groups, it was 12. Thus it is by no means true that equalizing as far as possible environmental factors which are believed to influence IQ eliminates black-white differences. These are slightly reduced for low status groups, but not for high status groups where they may in fact be accentuated. These facts do not accord well with the environmentalist hypothesis. But what may give readers sympathetic to this hypothesis most to think about will undoubtedly be the fact that the mean IQ of low status whites is actually 3 points above that of high status blacks. In other words, when environmental factors allegedly determining IQ favor the Negro group, they still perform less well than (disadvantaged) whites. Shuey comments on these various findings: "It is probable that the home, neighborhood, and school environment of the white and colored lower-class children tested are more nearly alike in their stimulating qualities (*i.e.* culture-enriching experiences provided) than are the home, neighborhood, and school environments of the white and colored upper and middle-class children; but it seems improbable that upper and middle-class colored children would have no more cultural opportunities provided them than white children of the lower and lowest class."

Shuey offers two possible explanations of these findings. The first is that "status-bearing positions open to Negroes in the United States have not required as high a level of intelligence as the much larger number of status-bearing positions open to whites. If this is true, they have not served equally as selective agents in recruiting the most able coloreds from the laboring class as is true with whites. The continual drawing of the more intelligent from the lower classes would in time produce a difference in the mental test scores of the divergent classes; if this drain is not equally present in the colored and white races one would expect greater differences in the testing of high-status groups and lesser differences when low-status groups are compared." The second is that "the disadvantaged living in integrated neighborhoods may not be equally representative of their respective racial groups. Living in these mixed neighborhoods being more prestigious for colored than for whites, a form of selective migration may be presumed to operate, 'positively' for the Negroes and 'negatively' for the whites. If this hypothesis is correct, it would account for the leveling tendencies observed in the test performances of the two lower-class groups whenever the samples tested are drawn from mixed neighborhoods." These explanations seem reasonable, but whether or not they prove correct, it seems certain that whenever blacks and whites are compared with respect to IQ, obvious differences in socio-economic status, education, and similar factors do not affect the observed inferiority of the blacks very much.

We must conclude from this survey of the evidence that American Negroes on the average score something like 15 points of IQ below whites, with the southern Negroes showing a greater gap, and the northern Negroes a slighter one. These differences are sometimes expressed in terms of "overlap," and it may be useful to introduce this concept into our discussion.

By overlap is meant the percentage of Negroes' scores that equals or exceeds the mean test score of the compared white group, *i.e.* the proportion of Negroes having scores on IQ tests equal to or above the white mean. For school children, the average overlap is approximately 12% (primary schools); for high school students (secondary school) it is approximately 10%. At the college level, overlap is 7%. This gives us an average over all groups of 11%, with overlap steadily decreasing as higher levels of scholastic attainment are being reached. Thus about one in ten Negroes scores as high or higher than the average white. This statistic is, of course, only another way of presenting the self-same data, but it is perhaps somewhat more vivid and easily intelligible for non-statisticians than the (equivalent) statement that Negroes score one standard deviation below whites.

THIS PARTICULAR STATISTIC has been criticized by several writers, on the grounds that it exaggerates the inferiority of Negroes' scores. Unsophisticated readers are likely to run away with the impression that the curve of distribution of Negroes' scores overlaps with that of whites' scores only to the extent of some 10%, and this of course is quite untrue. After all, if some 90% of Negroes score below the white average, so do some 50% of whites! Consider Figure 1, which shows the actual distribution of IQ's for whites and a southern Negro sample, *i.e.* a sample which shows a greater difference than would be found with northern, or mixed northern and southern Negroes. The "overlap," as defined in the preceding paragraph is obviously very small, amounting to less than 10%. But the overlap in the sense of distribution coincidence is quite large—only a minute proportion of Negroes score lower than the lowest white, and only a small proportion of whites score better than the highest-scoring Negro. It would seem that the term "overlap", used in its technical sense, is indeed misleading and gives an impression of Negro inferiority in no way justified by the facts. Naturally writers are entitled to use descriptive statistics in any way they like; but there is no obvious advantage to the "overlap" concept as compared to the much more widely used standard deviation, and the very name "overlap" clearly misleads the casual reader who is unacquainted with statistical detail, and gives an erroneous impression.

The facts regarding white and black comparisons on IQ scores are serious enough without exaggerating the observed differences in this manner. The excuse that the term is in fact usually carefully defined before being used is not good enough. Simple statements about overlap being only 10% are often repeated in newspapers and other sources without careful definition, and many readers will therefore obtain quite the wrong view. Writers on the subject would seem to have a social duty to guard against misrepresentation, as well as being accurate in their statements. In this sense facts in a socially sensitive area are undoubtedly different to facts in other, not so sensitive areas where the use of arbitarary statistics, provided they are properly defined, is less dangerous.

Another way of looking at the facts—favored by those who would like play down, rather than up, the marked disparity in scores between whites and blacks—is to consider the probability of diagnosing a person's race from knowing his

IQ, and nothing else about him. As already pointed out, the improvement above chance is only some 5%. (The actual figure depends somewhat on precise assumptions made, base rates used, etc., but is certainly unimpressive whichever way you look at it.) Again, statistically speaking this figure is quite all right, in the sense of being accurate and not contravening any rules of inference; however, it is somewhat unrealistic as no one would ever be likely to diagnose a person's race on the basis of his IQ! Being quite unusual and unorthodox as a statistic, this figure is difficult to interpret, even by experienced psychometrists, and has no obvious advantage over the more usual standard deviation. It may easily give the wrong impression by seeming to suggest that the observed differences are much smaller than they are—just as "overlap" may suggest the contrary. There is no obvious advantage to either type of statistic, and it might be suggested that both be dropped in future writings. Both are misleading, though on different sides of the great divide. They have been discussed here only to warn the reader of the dangers attending their use.

WHAT, THEN, MAY WE CONCLUDE from this array of facts? Shuey ends her book with a splendid "concluding statement," a single sentence snaking its way over thirty-five lines of print. It may be useful to quote her, as no doubt she knows more about this subject than any other writer living at present (although whether we can agree with her or not will be the subject of another chapter). This is what she says:

"The remarkable consistency in test results, whether they pertain to school or pre-school children, to children between ages 6 to 9 or 10 to 12, to children in Grades 1 to 3 or 4 to 7, to high school or college students, to enlisted men or officers in training in the Armed Forces—in World War I, World War II, or the post-Korean period—to veterans of the Armed Forces, to homeless men or transients, to gifted or mentally deficient, to delinquent or criminal; the fact that differences between colored and white are present not only in the rural and urban south, but in the border and northern states; the fact that the colored pre-school, school, and high school pupils living in northern cities tested as far below the southern urban white children as they did below the white in the northern cities; the fact that relatively small average differences were found between the IQ's of northern-born and southern-born Negro children in northern cities; the fact that Negro school children and high school pupils have achieved average IQ's slightly lower in the past twenty years than between 1921 and 1944; the tendency toward greater variability among whites; the tendency for racial hybrids to score higher than those groups described as, or inferred to be, unmixed Negro; the evidence that the mean overlap is between 7 and 13%; the evidence that the tested differences appear to be greater for logical analysis, abstract reasoning, and perceptual-motor tasks than for practical and concrete problems; the evidence that the tested differences may be a little less on verbal than on non-verbal tasks; the indication that the colored elementary or high school pupil has not been adversely affected in his tested performance by the presence of a white examiner; the indication that Negroes may have a greater sense of personal worth than whites, at least at the elementary, high school, and college levels; the unproved and probably erroneous assumption that Negroes have been less well motivated on tests than whites; the fact that differences were reported in practically all of the studies in which the cultural environment of the whites appeared to be similar in richness and complexity to that of the Negroes; the fact that in many comparisons, including those in which the colored had appeared to best advantage, Negro subjects have been either more representative of their racial group or more highly selected than the comparable whites; all taken together, inevitably point to the presence of native differences between Negroes and whites as determined by intelligence tests."

5

CHANGING HUMAN NATURE

DO THE FACTS really point "inevitably" to the presence of native differences between blacks and whites in the determination of IQ test results?

This conclusion has been supported by many experts but has also been criticized. It will be our task in this chapter to take a closer look at the rationale underlying the various approaches outlined in the previous chapters, and attempt to come to some rational conclusion about the present state of this problem. Such rational conclusions are not made easier by the highly emotional tone of some of the criticisms hurled at writers who venture to support the view that a genetic factor may be implicated. This is clearly a complex and difficult field, and it is possible to hold opposing views on many aspects of the problem without being motivated by doubtful social and political beliefs. *Argumenta ad hominem* can be hurtful, though they may please the committed. They have no logical force, and only make more difficult the task of making sense out of the host of available facts. Let us assume that all those who have taken a serious interest in this problem are motivated by honorable and praiseworthy desires to get at the truth, and let us simply look at the evidence, rather than at the people proposing and opposing various theories. The value of their arguments is not affected by their motivation, even if we could ever hope to know what that motivation really was.

We find that there are two main types of explanation for the undoubted inferiority of American Negroes on IQ tests as compared with American whites. Environmentalists tend to explain this inferiority in terms of deprivation of some kind or other. They appeal to the poorer environment of the black, the poorer education given him, the poorer nutrition he and his parents receive, the lack of books, of parental encouragement, of cultural traditions, and many other environmental factors which are spelled out in detail in the writings (particularly) of many sociologists. Environmentalists consider that these factors by themselves are sufficient to explain all the observed differences, without having to appeal, in addition, to genetic causes. They assert that the gene-pools of the two groups in question are identical, as far as determination of mental abilities are concerned. Adherents of this belief do not accept the genetic evidence presented (for reasons to be discussed presently) and believe that changes in the environmental circumstances holding down the Negro would produce an increase in his IQ scores which would bring him up to the level of the average white.

The alternative to this type of explanation is *not*, as is widely believed, a purely hereditarian position which would account for all the observed phenomena in terms of genetic factors alone. No serious psychologist or geneticist has ever, to my knowledge, put forward such a view. And indeed a theory of this kind would run foul of the most elementary tenets of genetic science, with its stress on the difference between genotype and phenotype. The alternative is, rather, some form of *interactionist* belief according to which genetic factors, interacting with environmental ones, are active in producing the observed racial differences. This, of course, suggests immediately that we ought to find out the relative importance of these factors, however rough and ready our first groping guesses might turn out to be. When the term "hereditarian" view, or position, or theory, is used in this book, or in other books written on the subject, *it always refers to this interactionist position.* The term "hereditarian" is simply taken as a shorthand reference to the clumsy phrase "heredity and environment acting together to produce the observed phenotype."

Given that these two positions are being defended by various academic writers ranging from sociologists and psychologists to geneticists and other types of biologists, can we conclude that either position has been clearly and completely established, without any doubt whatever? The answer to such a question, as already indicated on an earlier page, must inevitably be "no." Science does not work with absolute certainties, and anyone claiming that such certainty attaches to his position is clearly more optimistic than wise. Thus when critics claim that the evidence for the involvement of genetic factors is less than conclusive, they are right. No such conclusive evidence would be expected, and claims that it existed would have to be regarded with extreme suspicion. They are also right, as already pointed out, when they say that the hereditarian explanation is only a theory. All generalizations in science have the status of a theory, and the hereditarian theory does not differ in this from widely held theories in physics or chemistry or astronomy.

What the critics seldom add is that the environmentalist explanation is also only a theory. However plausible it may sound at first sight to the man in the street, it has exactly the same status scientifically as the hereditarian explanation— both are alternative theories, and require careful empirical study to substantiate or infirm their respective claims. It is thus quite wrong to regard the theoretical status of the hereditarian hypothesis as a criticism, although many laymen seem to accept it as such, no doubt identifying "theory" with "airy-fairy speculation." When it is realized that both positions are in fact theories, it will be obvious that both are in the same boat, and that the crucial thing to do is to consider to what extent these different theories are able to account for the observed facts.

THERE ARE TWO MAIN LINES of argumentation here, and it is important to realize this. Some critics (particularly geneticists) have been content to look at one line of argument, the purely genetic. They conclude (rightly) that this is not conclusive, and then argue that the "Jensenist heresy" is mistaken. As we shall see, this is not so. However, let us consider for a moment the importance, as well as the insufficiency, of the argument from genetics.

This is based on the facts outlined in an earlier chapter, showing that within carefully specified white populations, at a carefully specified moment in history (to wit—the present) intelligence differences between persons making up this population are determined more strongly by genetic factors than by environmental ones. Computations making use of many divergent sources of evidence converge on a figure of something like 80% being contributed by nature, 20% by nurture, with interaction effects being rather unimportant. These facts and conclusions are not really in dispute, although some writers would put the figure somewhat lower than 80%, others somewhat higher. Such arguments about improving estimates of a quantitative kind are common in all branches of science. They do not invalidate the basic hypothesis, and I can only report that among experts the conclusion I mentioned above is pretty universally accepted, and we may provisionally use it to build up our first argument.

The argument is simply that this discovery of strong genetic involvement in the determination of individual differences in IQ between members of a given population is an essential precondition for going on to argue in favor of the genetic determination (in part at least) of racial differences in IQ. For clearly if all the within-race differences could be accounted for in environmental terms, we would have no business to look further than that in our search for between-race differences. Thus the discovery of within-race genetic factors determining IQ differences is a *necessary*, but not a *sufficient* condition of accepting the genetic argument as applied to between-race differences.

Can we go beyond this and argue that genetic studies of the kind discussed in an earlier study give *direct* support to the hereditarian position? The answer must, I think, be in the negative. The two populations involved (black and white) are separate populations, and none of the studies carried out on whites alone, such as twin studies, are feasible. We cannot expect ever to find in real life the happy outcome attending the well known Miss Starkey, who foolishly married a darkie; the two, for their sins, had three pairs of twins, one white, one black, and one khaki. In any case, even if we could find such a paragon, the within-pair comparison would still be between white and white, or black and black, or khaki and khaki!

The direct argument is weakened even more by the fact that no proper twin studies, or other genetic studies of a similar kind, have been done with Negro subjects. Practically all our evidence comes from whites. This can, to be sure, be remedied. It is hoped that one of the consequences of the commotion caused by Jensen's book will be a renewed interest in the empirical studies which alone can refute or support his claims. But the fact remains that we do not know exactly what would be found, and even if Negroes showed precisely the same kind of within-race genetic determination of IQ as do whites, nevertheless there is no absolutely compelling argument from this to a between-race comparison. What is worse, it is difficult to see how an experiment could be devised, at the present state of knowledge, which would get over this difficulty. A suggestion has been made in the last chapter which might give fairly conclusive results, involving the serological and morphological analysis of white ancestry admixture in samples of Negroes. No doubt human ingenuity will eventually solve this particular problem, and come up with suggestions which might give us a more direct answer, in genetic terms, than we can hope for at present. Nevertheless, critics are perfectly right in saying that the genetic evidence existing at the moment is not conclusive.

However, it constitutes presumptive evidence which is quite strong, and cannot be disregarded. Any argument aimed at disavowing the genetic evidence runs into difficulties which may be more disturbing to the white-black hypothesis than anything postulated in this book. To suggest that the genetic determination of IQ, so strongly supported by research in white subjects, would not obtain with black subjects is ultimately to argue that there are far more profound, qualitative genetic differences between whites and blacks than have ever been postulated by Jensen or other geneticist writers on the subject. The argument against Jensen thus proves too much. It does not support an egalitarian hypothesis at all, but rather postulates even more decisive racial differences in the genetic determination of IQ. This is hardly what those proposing these arguments intend; but it is the logical outcome of the discussion.

WHEN WE LOOK AT the environmentalist theory, we find that while at first glance it appears sensible, reasonable, and down-to-earth, it is by no means as clear-cut as one might wish. Mention has already been made of the contradictions often discovered in the argument when it is applied to different types of empirical observation. We will find time and time again that this is by no means an isolated instance, but that the environmentalistic theory is in reality too vague to be properly tested at all. Let us consider a few facts and see how well the theory stands up to scrutiny, taking it in its most obvious form as expressed at the beginning of this chapter.

Can we account, in these terms, for the fact that when whites and blacks are matched on education, socio-economic status, and living area, differences are only slightly reduced as far as IQ is concerned? Or the even more damaging fact that higher-class Negroes, when compared with lower-class whites, are still inferior in IQ? Note that all the factors which are customarily suggested to produce Negro inferiority (educational provision, socio-economic status, area of residence) in actual fact strongly favor the Negroes involved in the comparison as opposed to the whites who are the "culturally disadvantaged" in this comparison.

Environmentalists sometimes suggest additional factors, quite different to those mentioned before, such as "lack of drive," or "feelings of racial inferiority," as accounting for the observed differences. (Note that these are brought in to explain away the failure of the original hypothesis, which is of course the one which has the popular appeal as being more or less "self-evidently" true.) The empirical evidence quoted in the last chapter does not support these factors either, and, as we shall see, direct examination of such alleged causes fails to show any evidence for their existence. In any case, to suggest that middle-class Negroes, who have had to fight hard (probably harder than whites) for their position, have no "drive" is, on the face of it, absurd. One might with much more justice argue that they must have had a lot more drive than most whites—certainly than those who remain in the lower class groups.

Take another example, also already mentioned, namely that of the IQ test performance of (American) Indians. It will be remembered that on the twelve most widely used sociological and psychological indices of socio-economic and educational status these were as far inferior to Negroes, as were Negroes to whites; yet the Indians performed better than the Negroes. It seems very difficult to explain this result away on grounds of "lack of drive" and "feelings of inferiority." Indians are renowned for their apathy, and share any "feelings of inferiority" with Negroes. Both races are discriminated against, with the Indians probably even worse off than the Negroes. Why then are the Indians not as far below the Negroes, as the Negroes are below the whites? Environmentalist theory does not provide an answer.

Sometimes environmentalists take the position that the "culture-biased" IQ tests used are at fault; we have already looked at this point briefly. But if this bias is responsible for Negro inferiority, why does it not work against other racial groups, like the Asians tested in California? They are inferior to whites on socio-economic and educational grounds, although not as much as the Negroes; but they nevertheless do as well as the whites, and even better when tests involving abstract reasoning are concerned. (One might advance the argument that perhaps racially orientals are superior to whites on IQ performance; I shall refrain from pursuing this point!) Cultural bias in "white IQ tests" has clearly not put oriental subjects off. Why should it affect Negroes so strongly, who after all have shared the white culture for much longer, and who are perhaps more closely integrated with it?

BUT THESE ARGUMENTS are perhaps indirect. It is useful to look at another racial group, the Mexicans living in California. These are well below the Negroes in socio-economic status and educational facilities; in IQ tests they score rather better than Negroes. (This failure of Mexican-Americans to score well below the Negroes poses another problem for the environmentalists; we will return later to this point.) But what is of particular interest in this connection is the *pattern* of scores obtained when Mexican and Negro children are given different kinds of IQ test, ranging from the most culturally dependent to the most culture fair. It has already been explained that no test can hope to be completely culture free or even culture fair; but tests can be designed to differ significantly with respect to the amount of cultural background and information required to succeed in it. On the environmental hypothesis, we would expect culturally deprived groups, of low socio-economic and educational status, to do less well on the more culturally dependent tests, and better on the more culture fair tests. This is precisely what we find with Mexican-American children; for them, therefore, the environmental hypothesis is strongly supported. But exactly the opposite is found for Negro children. For them the culture fair tests (involving abstract reasoning to a high degree) result in comparatively lower scores than do the more culture-bound tests. This result seems pretty conclusive, particularly when taken together with the finding, already discussed in the last chapter, that Negroes are in anything less inferior in verbal tests (depending on cultural influences) than on non-verbal and perceptual-motor tests (which are not so dependent).

The argument may benefit from quoting one or two actual examples; I have taken the first from one of Jensen's own studies. He argues that test difficulty may be varied in two ways. We can vary it by changing the rarity of the item content. Take a picture vocabulary test, in which a picture is shown and the subject has to pick out the correct descriptive noun from several choices. *Dog* is easy, *aardvark* is difficult; not because it is more difficult to form an association between picture and name in the case of the latter, but because both animal and name are more rarely encountered. Thus, a picture vocabulary test is closely culture-bound; those items which are rarely encountered in our culture are difficult, those which are frequently found are easy. Environmental influences, acquainting the child with these items up the scale, would seem relatively important, and the only ability required would seem to be associative. On the other hand, items such as those printed in Figure 6 derive their difficulty from their relative complexity; all the elements entering into them are equally familiar to the subject, and do not affect the difficulty. It is tests of this kind which are relatively culture fair.

Consider now the results of administering two tests to

white, Negro, and Mexican-American children from six to twelve years of age. One was the Peabody Picture Vocabulary test, the other the Progressive Matrices test, a test similar in kind to the items given in our Figure 6. We thus have a

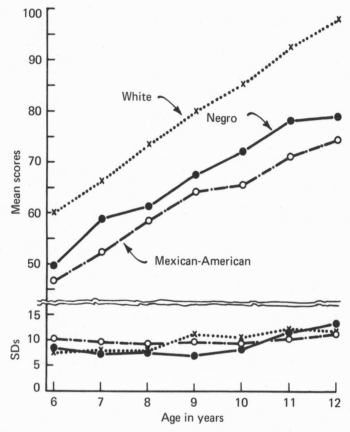

11 Scores of white, Negro, and Mexican-American children at various ages on the Peabody Picture Vocabulary Test, a culture-dependent test of IQ. Note the superiority of the Negroes to the Mexican-Americans. (The bottom of the diagram shows the standard deviation of the various groups.)

strongly culture-bound test (the picture vocabulary) and a reasonably culture fair test (the matrices). How do the children perform? According to their socio-economic status, the Mexican-Americans should be bottom, Negroes intermediate, and whites top. This is indeed found with the Peabody test (Figure 11) but not with the matrices test. On the former the Negroes are clearly superior, on the latter the Mexicans.

Jensen continues his analysis by showing that when children are equated with respect to their picture vocabulary scores, then Mexican-Americans score higher on the matrices than do white or Negro children; this is consistent with the cultural deprivation hypothesis. But the Negroes go in exactly the opposite direction. They score lower than Mexicans or whites! In other words, this test is capable of demonstrating cultural effect on IQ scores (as shown by the results achieved by the Mexicans) but it fails to demonstrate any such effects in the case of the Negroes. Negro pupils do better, relative to whites and Mexican-Americans, on the *more* culture-loaded than on the *less* culture-loaded test. It would seem very difficult to account for these findings about the Negro children in purely environmental terms.

POSSIBLY EVEN MORE impressive is another of Jensen's studies. He tested large groups of white, Negro and Mexican-American children on a battery of tests. These were found (by statistical analysis) to fall into four quite separate and distinct factors or groups: (1) Verbal IQ and scholastic achievement tests; (2) Non-verbal IQ tests, like Raven's Matrices; (3) Rote memory tests; and (4) measures of socio-economic status of the child's family. Scores on each of these factors are shown in Figure 12 for whites, Negroes, and Mexican-Americans separately. Each racial group is represented by children from the fourth, fifth and sixth grade, to show that results from one grade are replicable in the other grades. The following points should be noted: (1) Mexican-

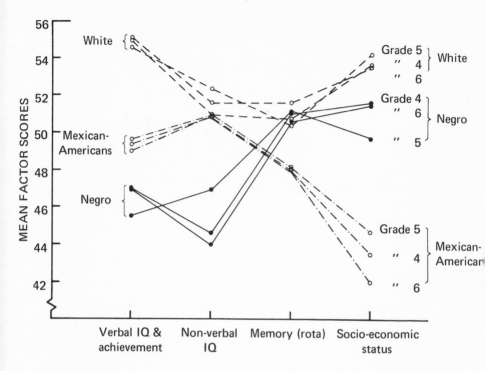

12 Graph showing the relative standing of white, black, and Mexican-American children from grades 4, 5 and 6 on four variables: socio-economic status, verbal IQ and school achievement, non-verbal (culture fair) IQ, and rote memory. Scores are calculated in such a way that the children's standing on any one factor is independent of that on other factors. Note that when children are thus equated for ability and school achievement, Mexican-Americans are much the lowest in socio-economic status, with whites and blacks nearly equal. Conversely, with socio-economic status held constant, whites and Mexican-Americans are equal on "culture fair" IQ, with Negroes well below. With non-verbal IQ and socio-economic status held constant, whites are superior to both Mexican-Americans and Negroes. These results suggest that Mexican-Americans are culturally deprived, and hence scholastically backward, but without any "culture fair" IQ deficit. Negroes, on the other hand, show much less evidence of cultural deprivation, but much lower "culture fair" IQ's.

The IQ Argument

American children are by far the lowest in socio-economic status, being over three times as much below the whites as are the Negroes. (This statistic does not take into account the additional fact, very important for school work, that English is the only language spoken in the child's home in 96.5% of white homes, 98.2% of Negro homes, but only in 19.7% of Mexican-American homes; in the last-mentioned homes, Spanish or some other foreign language is the only language spoken in 14.2% of all cases!) Thus, on an environmentalist hypothesis, Mexican-American children should do much worse than Negro children on IQ tests and school work.

(2) On tests of non-verbal intelligence, *i.e.* culture fair tests, Mexican-Americans are hardly inferior to whites. Both groups are markedly superior to Negroes.

(3) On verbal IQ and school achievement, Mexican-Americans are still superior to Negroes, although inferior to whites.

(4) On rote memory, Negroes are equal to whites, Mexican-Americans are inferior in both groups. These results would seem to defy explanation in purely environmentalistic terms. Jensen adds that in case unsophisticated readers might think that these surprising results are in some way due to a statistical legerdemain, a simple plot for one culture fair test (Raven's Matrices) might dispel this notion; this diagram is given as Figure 13. The intermediate position of the Mexican-Americans, in spite of their gross inferiority in point of socio-economic status, is obvious.

ALL THESE ARGUMENTS somehow involve racial overtones, and seem to argue for the intellectual inferiority, or superiority, of one race compared with another. Yet, on the assumptions which have governed our argument, it should be possible to find within the white race, groups of people—interbreeding and subject to common selection factors and policies—which would have a different gene pool from other groups, and from which they were relatively isolated. Such differences might then show themselves in a differential IQ

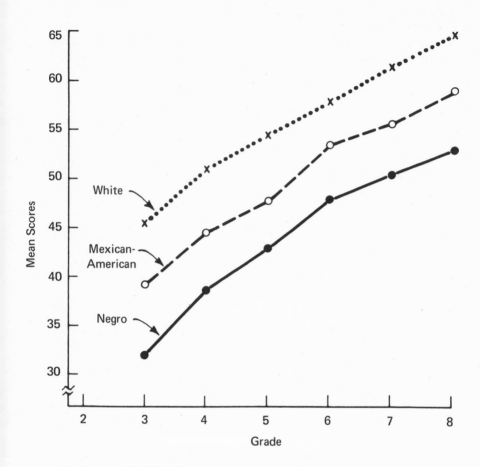

13 Scores of white, Mexican-American, and Negro children on the Progressive Matrices test, a culture fair type of IQ test. Note that although Mexican-American children are lower in socio-economic status than Negro children, they score much higher than Negro children on this test. Compare these results with those recorded in Figure 12, where Negro children are superior to Mexican-American children on a culture dependent test of IQ. (Scores are given in terms of T-scores, *i.e.* having a mean of 50 and a standard deviation of 10.)

level. Such groups do exist. And their very existence strongly supports our argument—as well as demonstrating that it is not in any sense a racialist one. As an example, take the Irish. Here is a well defined, interbreeding population, isolated on an island, and thus removed from most sources of outbreeding, and certainly subject to historical processes which might be expected to have drawn away, over many centuries, the most able and adventurous of citizens to foreign countries. Under these circumstances (which in some ways are the opposite of those attending the selection of Negroes for shipment to the U.S.A., and their subsequent fate) we might expect a distinctly lower IQ level among the remaining Irish than would be found in other countries not subject to this particular selection process. Facts seem to confirm these hypotheses; Macnamara found the Irish to have IQ's which were not very different from those observed in American Negroes, and far below comparable English samples.

Macnamara suggests some plausible reasons why the observed figures might need some scaling up; but even when reasonable adjustments are made the differences between Irish and English results remain very large. These differences are difficult to trace to socio-economic causes, or educational ones, because there is not very much to choose between England and Ireland in these respects. Certainly, Irish children tested were superior to Negro children in these respects; yet they failed to score above the Negro mean on IQ tests. It seems reasonable to conclude that we are not dealing in these comparisons with racial difference (white *vs.* black) *per se*, but rather with special sub-groups within a given race. If we compared Negroes with Irish whites, we would conclude that whites and blacks had identical IQ's. What would happen if we compared American Negroes, or whites, with African Negroes we cannot tell, because (as explained before) there simply do not exist any tests which would make such a comparison possible. The important fact to be recognized is that we cannot meaningfully talk about the mean IQ of a whole race. What we are always concerned with is rather a relatively small sub-group (Irish whites, say, or American Negroes) from which it would not be admissible to argue to larger racial groups (all whites, say, or all Negroes). This restriction is important to bear in mind when assessing the results of the studies here reviewed. It should also be evident that even these smaller gene pools are not likely to be stationary, but are constantly changing in response to changed modes of selection, eugenic pressures (both positive and negative), and increasing racial mixtures. If similar comparisons had been carried out three hundred years ago with Irish and English children, quite likely no differences would have been found. If similar comparisons should be carried out in three hundred years' time with Negroes and white children in the U.S., quite possibly no difference will be found. We are taking cross-sections through history and geography. These do not enable us to forecast the future, or to reconstruct the past, without additional knowledge.

IT WILL HAVE BECOME CLEAR in our discussion that a recurring difficulty throughout has been the failure of environmentalists to make precise their hypotheses, and state them in testable terms. Another difficulty has been their failure to carry out experimental studies in which their theories could be subjected to some recognized process of verification or falsification. Much of the evidence detailed in the preceding chapters, in so far as it is relevant to the environmentalist position, is empirical but not experimental; the distinction is not absolute, of course, but worth noting.

As an example of the experimental approach, as opposed to the simply empirical-observational-statistical, consider an experiment reported by Jensen. In it he attempted to put to the test the environmentalist hypothesis, already considered to some extent, that Negroes are characterized by lack of motivation in the test-taking situation, fail to do themselves justice, and consequently score worse than their actual ability warrants. Jensen designed a test which contained two kinds of problems, one a true measure of abstract thinking ability, the other pure "busy work," and not correlated with IQ to any extent. The difference between these two kinds of problems was, however, not apparent to the persons tested—as far as they were concerned they were simply trying to find the solution to a single series of rather similar problems. Jensen argued that if Negroes failed to succeed in the abstract reasoning items (*i.e.* had lower IQ scores) because of lower motivation, then they should also do less well on the rote learning items. This, however, was not so. Negroes equalled whites on the rote learning items, but were well below them on the abstract reasoning items. This inferiority, therefore, cannot be argued away as being due to lack of motivation—no such lack was apparent on the rote learning items, and as already pointed out, to the testee the two kinds of items were not in any way distinguished or distinguishable. The same line of reasoning rules out other environmentalist hypotheses—discouragement by previous frustrating experiences in examination situations, feelings of inferiority, hostility to white examiners, etc. All these hypotheses would require Negroes to perform less well on the rote learning tasks, and their equal performance on them cannot be made to conform to any of these hypotheses.

It is not clear why environmentalists have failed to put their hypotheses forward in as explicit a manner as possible, make apparent the deductions which could be made from these hypotheses, and then test these deductions experimentally. If they had followed this line of work, which is clearly in accord with scientific practice, we would now know far more about the effects of environment than we do in fact know. It is possible—although I doubt it—that had they done this, we might now be in a position to refute the hereditarian theory on the basis of solid experimental work. As it is, most of the experimental and statistical-observational work so far has been done by hereditarians, who have been much less prone to rely on non-empirical modes of proof. Environmentalists must soon enter this arena if they do not wish their case to go by default.

ALL THE EVIDENCE TO DATE suggests the strong and indeed overwhelming importance of genetic factors in producing the great variety of intellectual differences which we observe in our culture, and much of the difference observed between certain racial groups. This evidence cannot be argued away by niggling and very minor criticisms of details which do not really throw doubts on the major points made in this book. What is required is more and better research, rigorous and careful theorizing, and a determined refusal to be blinded in one's conclusions by one's preconceptions. If environmentalists cannot provide this, then their case will be lost. Even if all this were forthcoming, it does not of course follow that their cause would prevail, but at least they would give it a proper chance. And in doing so they might furnish us with important information which might enable us to transcend the dilemma, by learning how to transform the environment in such a way as to alter the very contingencies of the problem with which we are wrestling.

This sentence requires some explanation for those who are not too familiar with genetics. Let us first consider an example, and then discuss its implications for the particular problem we are concerned with. Many people dislike hereditarian notions because they believe that these carry an implication of therapeutic nihilism. If something is innate, they are prone to argue, then there is by definition nothing you can do about it; let us rather concentrate on those aspects of the problem which we can affect in some way, *i.e.* the environmental ones. But this notion is mistaken. It assumes that what is true in one particular environment is universally true. As we have seen, that is not so. Change the environment in ways relevant to the problem, and you may change the phenotype in ways previously unexpected and impossible to predict without the requisite knowledge of just what it is that is being inherited.

Consider phenylketonuria, a well-known disease which affects about one European child in forty thousand (it is, interestingly, much rarer among Africans). This disorder causes mental defect, and it has been found that about one in every hundred patients in hospitals for severely mentally handicapped children suffers from it. This disorder is known to be inherited and is, in fact, due to a single recessive gene. The great majority of children suffering from it have a level of mental performance which is usually found in children half their age. These children can be distinguished from other mentally handicapped or from normal children by testing their urine, which yields a green-colored reaction with a solution of ferric chloride due to the presence of derivatives of phenylalanine. Here we have a perfect example of a disorder produced entirely by hereditary causes, where the cause is simple and well understood, and where the presence of the disorder can be determined with accuracy.

Does this discovery imply therapeutic nihilism? The answer is definitely no. Let us go on to demonstrate in what ways the gene actually produces the mental defect. It has been shown that children affected by phenylketonuria are unable to convert phenylalanine into tyrosine; they can only break it down to a limited extent. It is not clear why this should produce mental deficiency; but it seems probable that some of the incomplete breakdown products of phenylalanine are poisonous to the nervous system. Phenylalanine, fortunately, is not an essential part of the diet, provided that tyrosine is present in it. It is possible to maintain these children on a diet which is almost free of phenylalanine, thus eliminating the danger of poisoning to the nervous system. It has been found that when this method of treatment is begun in the first few months of life, there is a very good chance that the child may grow up without the mental handicap he would otherwise have encountered. In other words, by understanding the precise way in which heredity works, and by understanding precisely what it does to the organism, we can arrange a rational method of therapy which will make use of the forces of nature, rather than try to counteract them. Thus we are led to the paradoxical situation where *environmental* manipulation (withdrawal of food containing phenylalanine) becomes effective once the *hereditary* nature of the disorder is recognized, and a precise understanding of its mode of working has been achieved. These children live literally in a different environment, an environment not containing phenylalanine; in such an environment they are not handicapped and are equal to all other children.

Is there any likelihood of ever being able to boost IQ by such changes of environment? It has been suggested by South African doctors that putting expectant mothers in a decompression chamber before delivery raises the IQ of babies so delivered by something like 15 points. Unfortunately this is very unlikely to be true; but it is not impossible that a better understanding of the nature of intelligence may give into our hands methods of raising IQ's well above the limits which at present constrain us. Reference has already been made to studies showing it to be related to the electrical activity of the cortex as measured by evoked potentials. We are limited only by our ignorance, and this ignorance is likely to be prolonged if we accept without argument the unproven theories of environmentalists denying the importance of hereditary factors.

TO MOST PEOPLE, however, such developments lie in the future and may sound like science fiction. They are more likely to be concerned with the topic which lies at the heart of Jensen's book, namely the possibility of "compensatory education." This notion implies that by taking underprivileged children and giving their education a special boost, it may be possible to overcome the disadvantages of their poor educational and socio-economic environment and actually raise their IQ. As Jensen (and other critics) have pointed out, success so far has been less than impressive. One might in fact say that a great deal of money has been almost completely wasted, with very disappointing results. Jensen points out that this failure was predictable, and that these projects (like "Head Start" in the U.S.A.) were based on sociological and psychological theories which disregarded completely the evidence of hereditarian determination of IQ differences discussed by him, and in this book. This criticism is well taken. In what scientific field would large-scale programs be undertaken without previous detailed research to discover whether the methods used would actually work, and in complete contradiction to the best-established evidence in the field? These programs are political playthings. They have no scientific basis, have no recognizable or lasting effects on those exposed to them, and can only do a disservice to those truly eager to advance the status of the Negro race.

But the failure of those projects should not be interpreted to mean that better projects could not be designed, or that research should not be carried out in this field. Consider for instance the important work of Professor R. Heber of Wisconsin. He chose a group of Negro babies from severely underprivileged homes, with an expected mean IQ around 80. These were then taken from their homes every morning, brought to a special school where a trained female social worker spent the whole day with the child (one woman per child) trying to bring him on as fast as possible intellectually, by playing with him, talking to him, trying to teach him, and interacting constantly in such a way as to produce the maximum improvement in his mental state. In the evening the babies would be taken back to their mothers, who in turn would have received some help and advice on their many problems from the Project staff. Under these conditions the children simply shot ahead, reaching IQ's well above the 100 mark, thus excelling not only a matched Negro group but also normal white groups. In addition their whole behavior changed, and they became more talkative, forthcoming, and extroverted. These results apply to children who had reached the age of four at the time; and it would be very dangerous to extrapolate too far. It is well known that early advances are often not maintained into later adolescence, and IQ tests given at this age are poor predictors of adult IQ. Nevertheless the experiment is continuing and will be watched with great interest and hope by many psychologists.

Such environmental manipulation, even if it should prove successful, cannot of course be the answer. The cost is staggering, amounting to something like a million dollars a year, for just a hundred or so children. Furthermore, it does not go to the root of the Negro-white differential. It seems likely that white children would benefit equally, thus maintaining their superiority. But with all these qualifications the fact still remains that this experiment holds out the promise that, by transforming the environment in a manner going beyond anything attempted as yet, we may be able to raise IQ's generally to a degree which would make it possible for the average person to benefit from a university education which under present conditions would be well beyond his ability. Far more such research should be undertaken to make clear to us the limits of our ability at present to increase mental ability. The money wasted on "compensatory education" could have furnished us with a great deal of much-needed knowledge in this field—knowledge on which proper programs might have been based.

Note that there is nothing in Heber's experiment which contradicts the hereditarian position (always understanding this term to mean *the interaction between heredity and environment*). By introducing an environment never previously encountered he genuinely transcended the limitations of our present environment; no geneticist would have been able to predict what would happen. The generalizations we have made apply to our present time and condition; when these are no longer applicable, then these generalizations may or may not hold. For this reason extensions of the Heber experiment (to include white children of equally poor IQ expectations, and both white and Negro children of higher IQ expectations) are of the greatest importance and will add immeasurably to our knowledge and understanding.

The need, then, is for more and better research; only knowledge will set us free. And it is disappointing in the extreme that such august bodies as the American Academy of Science have come out against support of research in this field. Like the Aristotelian opponents of Galileo, they refuse to put the telescope to their eyes in case it might prove something they would rather not know. Grant-giving bodies, too, and government agencies have been rather shy of financing research in this field. It is always much easier to find money to waste on apparently benevolent projects which in actual fact are doomed to failure, than funds to spend on the much-needed research which alone will enable us to mount projects which will in actual fact do some good. The importance of research is still very poorly understood by politicians and civil servants. Those who suffer from all this are, of course, precisely those who can do least to correct it.

CAN WE, THEN, CHANGE human nature? This is one of those questions, like the one about the squirrel and the tree, where everything depends on one's understanding of the words involved. If we mean "Can we change the genotype?" then the answer at present is probably "No," although even here there are the beginnings of a scientific revolution which may in due course enable us to indulge in genetic engineering. But the time is not yet and for the present we must accept the genotype as we find it. But if we mean "Can we change the phenotype?" then the answer must of course be "Yes." Even our calculation that at present environmental influences contribute some 20% to the variability of human IQ makes it clear that this phenotype is already partly under environmental control. If Heber's experiment should prove to have lasting effects we would have further evidence in favor of our ability to manipulate the phenotype. What the limitations of this manipulation might be we simply do not know. Again, the needed research has just not been done—and the educational establishment shows very little sign of getting down to doing it. In this sense, however, there is no doubt that we can change human nature; all we need is greater scientific knowledge than we have at present.

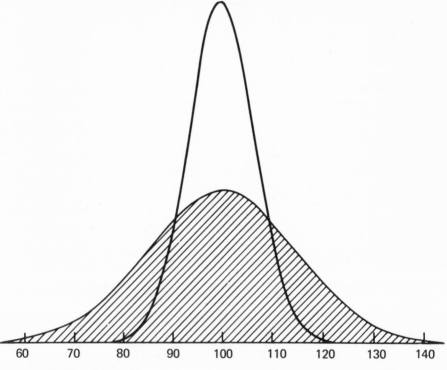

14 The heavy line shows what the distribution of IQ's would be theoretically if all genotypes were identical (*i.e.* everyone had identical heredity for intelligence) and all differences in IQ were due entirely to environmental differences. The shaded curve represents the normal distribution of IQ's in the present population.

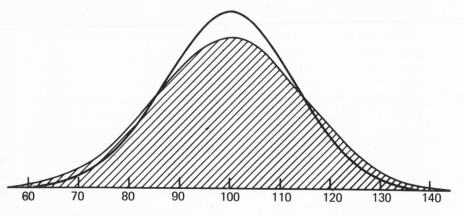

15 The heavy line shows what the distribution of IQ's would be theoretically if all variance due to environmental factors had been eliminated and all differences in IQ were due entirely to hereditarian influences. The shaded curve represents the normal distribution of IQ's in the present population.

Actually even the present margin of 20% environmental contribution gives us quite a wide range of "changeability" as far as IQ is concerned; this is well illustrated in Figures 14 and 15 (taken from Jensen). The former compares the range of IQ's actually encountered in a world like the present English or American cultures where heritability is approximately 80%, with the range that would be encountered if heredity treated everyone exactly alike and only environment produced differences in IQ. It will be seen that under those conditions the dullest would have IQ's of 80 or thereabouts, and the brightest IQ's of 120 or thereabouts, all due to environmental determinants similar to those encountered at present and without introducing the special conditions of Heber's experiment. Figure 15 shows the comparison of conditions as they are now, and conditions as they would be if environment was exactly alike for everyone and played no part at all in determining differences in IQ. It will be seen that eradicating all environmental influences would not greatly affect the distribution of IQ's.

The contrast shows quite clearly that even Heber's results, striking as they are, could still be accommodated within the confines of the present model. Gains of 30 points of IQ would take his subjects, who had an expectation of IQ's in the neighborhood of 80, up to 110 or thereabouts, even assuming that these gains could be consolidated and were not lost during later childhood and adolescence. Indeed, if the conditions under which these children normally grow up could be said to be the least stimulating normally encountered in our society, and those of Heber's experiment the most stimulating normally encountered in our society, then there would still be room for a further growth of 10 points within the confines of our hypothesis. Critics of the hereditarian hypothesis, which as we have often pointed out is really an interactionist hypothesis, tend to forget that this theory embodies a sizeable chunk of environmental influence; Figure 15 shows just how much leeway this affords us. Anyone favoring a purely environmentalist theory would have to demonstrate effects of environmental manipulation (of a kind normal in our society) which had effects greater than those for which provision is made in our model. No one has ever done this, and until it is done little credence attaches to speculative arguments about what might happen.

WHAT WE CAN DO at present is to make maximum use of the particular abilities which children possess, rather than put them all into a bed of Procrustes created by the assumption that genetically they are all equal in ability—indeed in all ability," Jensen has brought forward evidence to show that disadvantaged children are not inferior to high IQ children with respect to tests of what he calls "associative learning ability", while falling behind on tests of "conceptual learning ability" (see Figure 12). He suggests that in teaching different children we should make use of their strengths; where modern methods of teaching often stress conceptual abilities, this clearly favors the bright, high IQ child. He suggests experimenting with methods of teaching specially geared to the duller child's relatively high "associative learning ability." In this way he feels we might give this child a chance to reach much higher educational levels than it might otherwise be able to reach. This proposal has been caricatured as giving "inferior" education to black children as compared with white; but this is, of course, nonsense. In the first place what he says applies equally to the duller white child as to the duller black child; race is quite irrelevant here. And in the second place he is merely suggesting what every educationalist is trying to do—build upon abilities which are present in the child. Jensen may of course be mistaken in his analysis, and further research will no doubt tell us if this is so or not. But in principle it seems absurd to refuse to look at new methods of teaching a particular group of children, which might help them to reach much higher levels of performance, on the grounds that these methods contradict quite arbitrary principles which have never received any experimental support. Education has always suffered from its cult of fads. These change from decade to decade, being replaced not by methods based on experimentally established truth but by other fads equally unlikely to succeed or last for any length of time. We have finally reached the position where some of our future teachers, being trained in Colleges of Education, are unable to spell properly or write English grammatically. What more do we need to demonstrate that our present methods are, to say the least, unequal to what is demanded of them?

Educationalists have always shown to an extreme degree the besetting sin of many people who wish to change the world: the refusal to acknowledge the diversity of human nature. Bright children need different approaches to teaching compared to dull ones, extroverted children to introverted ones, emotionally labile children to emotionally stable ones. It is simply not meaningful to ask general questions, such as "Is streaming in schools good or bad for children?" This depends on the children, the attitudes and values of the teachers, as well as their training. It depends on the views of the parents, the curriculum used and the criteria adopted—there is no single answer to the question. It has been shown by Dr. R. Holden that when experimental tests are carried out to compare the results of streaming and not streaming, on the same set of children, extroverted children react differently to introverted ones, a difference which is further confounded according to whether your criteria are social or educational. The notion that there is one best method of teaching, one single method which is applicable to all children regardless of personality, ability, or circumstances, dies hard. Recognition that the very notion is an insult to human individuality seems a necessary preliminary to any improvement in our system of teaching. I can see nothing wrong in adapting teaching methods to human differences. If Jensen's suggestion should prove to raise the quality of the work done by duller children and bring it closer to the level reached by the brighter ones, then I can see no objection to adopting the methods suggested, at least until better ones become available. To refuse to do this seems doctrinaire in the very worst sense, jeopardizing the future of the children concerned for arbitrary ideological reasons. We will not succeed in changing human nature by refusing to recognize facts.

6

THE SOCIAL RESPONSIBILITY
OF SCIENCE

FOR CENTURIES the black man has been oppressed, enslaved, exploited, vilified, and held in contempt; those whose forefathers were responsible for these crimes, and those who still continue to deny the black man equality and justice, bear a heavy burden of guilt. If, as the data suggest, Negroes in the U.S.A. show some genetic influence on their low IQ's, this may very well be due to the after-effects of some of the crimes committed on their ancestors—just as the Irish show a similar low IQ, probably because of the oppression they uffered for so many centuries at the hands of the English. The reasons for the present state of affairs can only be guessed at; the facts themselves are not really in dispute. American Negroes score something like 15 points of IQ below white Americans, and even when environmental, educational and socio-economic influences are rendered as equal as possible, this difference shows little sign of diminishing very much. There are good (although not conclusive) reasons for assuming that a considerable portion of this difference is genetic in origin; no precise estimates can be attempted at this point. When environmentalistic hypotheses are tested, they fail to stand up to scrutiny or experiment. If environmental causes are all-important they have certainly not yet been isolated, or shown to be so. Lack of properly conceived research does not enable us at present to make more than guesses at the methods which we might use to introduce "compensatory programs" which would really have a measurable effect on Negro (or disadvantaged white) IQ.

All this is of course completely irrelevant, as already pointed out, to the question of segregation. Human beings have human rights, irrespective of their IQ, and the fact that Negroes show some degree of genetic inferiority in respect to this particular measure (which is *not* a measure of human worth, but only of capacity for abstract thought, educability, and similar abilities) does not carry with it any implications whatever favoring differential schooling. The continued segregation of Negroes in the U.S.A., the still-prevalent restrictions on their employment and advancement, and the widespread prejudice against their political emancipation are inexcusable, and obtain no support from such data as those surveyed in this book. The educational problem which faces us is that of the low-IQ pupil, whether black or white, and its solution must be found irrespective of color. Every human being has the right to an education that brings out the best that is within him; his color or sex or religion must under no circumstances be allowed to interfere with this fundamental principle.

Such a right, however, must not be misinterpreted to read that everyone must be given identical primary, secondary and advanced education. The majority of youngsters have neither the ability nor the desire for academic training in universities and colleges (at least if those universities maintain genuinely high standards), and it is not unreasonable to demand of those who do express a wish for such education some evidence of both ability and motivation. This evidence should be forthcoming from black and white alike; here, too, absolute equality is essential. This has one implication which may not appeal to American Negroes, namely the implication that no *inverted* racist policy should be allowed to operate, setting lower entrance requirements for Negroes, or introducing a quota system to make sure that blacks and whites attend university in proportion to their numerical strength in the country or state. However much one may sympathize with Negro demands of this kind, they infringe the general rule laid down above, and are racist in nature. If accepted, such demands would mean that a well qualified, high IQ white student would be debarred from attending university in order to allow a less well qualified, lower IQ black student to take his place *on purely racial grounds.* This is unacceptable in principle. It is also likely to have certain undesirable consequences—the standards of teaching would have to drop drastically to take account of the newcomers with low IQ and low educational attainment, while the newcomers would find the going extremely difficult and might only be soured by failure to reach the high standards required in our universities. Racial grounds for acceptance and rejection are unacceptable regardless of which race is favored; it is the principle which is wrong. Each person must be considered on his merits; color of skin is not a merit—nor of course a demerit.

This does not mean that something should not be done to recompense the Negro within the limits of the possible for all the sufferings that whites have inflicted on his race. I would argue (and this of course is a personal opinion, not the results of scientific research) that if we accept the proposition that the available evidence points to some degree of genetic determination of Negro inferiority in IQ, then we are in duty bound to try and set up countervailing environmental pressures which would as far as possible redress this balance and bring the Negro up to white standards. The difficulty, as already pointed out several times, is our ignorance and lack of proper research. We have neglected this field in fear of what we might find, and as a result our pious hopes and benevolent desires cannot be put into effect—we just don't know how we could raise the level of Negro intelligence, or even how we would improve his school performance. Those with an urgent wish to do good, or with political commitments in this area, are only too eager to embark on costly projects which, if past history is anything to go by, are doomed to failure. Social science has been underfinanced for so many years that no quick and easy remedies are likely to be forthcoming even if we did undertake the needed research. If we are serious about our desire to help the black man to come into his own, and to redress to some extent the balance our ancestors have so fatally upset, then we have simply no alternative but to set in motion properly conceived, large scale schemes of psychological, sociological, and educational research which may, in due course, give us the answers which at the moment we so patently lack. And these answers will of course equally benefit white children of low IQ and poor educational attainment (who after all outnumber black children of low IQ and poor educational attainment). The racial issue in this connection is nothing but a red herring. Let us get away from rhetorical discussion, name-calling, and philosophical speculation, and get down to the work needed to put into effect what all people of good intention desire— the advancement and rehabilitation of the under-privileged.

AND SO WHAT OF the Jensenist heresy? We can now see it as a nonsense, an alogy, an extravagance, a farrago, a mare's nest, an amphigouri; the invention of people whose failure to read, mark and understand Jensen's clear and considered text led them to put forth a version of their own which rightly attracted a great deal of criticism. But what they said is not what Jensen said. He carefully put in all the qualifications which scientific honesty demanded, while they left them out in their accounts.

The Jensenist heresy turns out to be nothing but purest orthodoxy; it has been turned into heresy by those who popularized and criticized his views without taking the trouble to understand them first of all. The facts, as we see them now, support his tentative and carefully worded conclusions. All he finally concluded was that there is a good deal of evidence (which he never considered conclusive) to show that white-black IQ differences were in part genetically caused, and that sufficient knowledge had been accumulated to make it clear that more incisive research could now be undertaken to gain further insight into this important question. He also concluded that compensatory programs had failed (which is universally acknowledged to be true) and suggested a possible cause, namely the neglect of just those facts which have concerned us in this book. Finally, he offered some suggestions, based upon important and novel experimental research of his own, which might lead to an improvement in the education of duller and disadvantaged children of all races.

The message, in this case, clearly is not the medium. The message has been lacerated, ruptured, crunched, mangled, scrambled, hackled, shivered, quartered, divellicated, minced, pulverized and comminuted to suit the needs of the mass media. Readers who wish to form a proper judgment on his contribution to this topic are advised to read his own words. The Jensenist heresy never existed. Let us get on with the business of getting to grips with the true issues.

What are the true issues? They center on the problem of educating the less able, less academic, less educable generally in such a way that they are enabled to play a proper part in the economic, industrial and commercial life of the nation, instead of being condemned to blind-alley jobs, unskilled labor, or the dole; and also of educating them in such a way that they are enabled to enjoy the abundant leisure which we are told is just around the corner for everyone. To be sure, this is a general problem, not one limited to, or even particularly linked with, the color question. It is doubtful if anyone familiar with what goes on in our schools, or what comes out of our schools by way of finished product, can honestly say that we have even begun to attack this problem seriously. Bored youngsters, eager to leave at the first opportunity; boys and girls almost illiterate, unable to write or spell or read anything but comics: these are the proud products of an educational system which flits from fad to fad without any basis in solid research, or proper understanding of the processes involved in learning, or the bases of motivation. From "formal training" to "free expression" educationalists have made arbitrary and purely *a priori* choices among alternatives none of which had any support from experimental psychology. No wonder none of them worked in practice! This probably does not matter so much for the bright child; his natural intelligence can overcome almost any system of training and education invented by the perverse minds of school teachers. It is the dull ones, who need support most, who suffer. The wonder is not that they run wild, but rather that they tolerate so patiently what is done to them in the name of education.

This, then, is a general problem, and even if, as we have shown, a higher proportion of blacks than whites is to be found in the "under 90 IQ" group, this hardly makes it a racial problem. It is considered that any big industrial concern should finance research into the processes used by it to the tune of between 1% and 5% of its turnover in order to remain competitive. Education does not finance research into education at a rate even one-hundredth of that. Until it does it is unlikely that these problems will be solved.

IF ALL THIS IS SO, why then are studies like those reported in this book important? If the fundamental problem is not a racial one, and if children and adults alike are to be judged in terms of their particular pattern of abilities, personality traits, and other individual characteristics rather than in terms of their color, why worry about the genetic or environmentalistic determination of IQ?

The answer must be in terms of the most promising avenues of research (and public policy) to be pursued. If the environmentalists were right, then it would be easy—or relatively so—to pull up the disadvantaged to the level of the advantaged; "Head Start" would make sense, and so would all the other programs of compensatory education. Less sanguine views about the possibilities opened up by these programs have unfortunately been only too well justified by the final outcome. Clearly, methods which make sense to the man in the street, and to sociologists and educationists ignorant of the biological facts, do not work. We have to go back to the drawing board and start again at the beginning. We already know a few things, and these few things suggest an entirely different strategy for our endeavors to introduce a meaningful program of compensatory education. The position is the same as in the case of phenylketonuria (only of course much more complex). Consider what nonsense any program of "compensatory education" would have made of efforts to bring these defective children up to normality! Only the realization of the genetic origin of the disorder enabled us to   investigate the precise nature of what it was that had been inherited, and to take environmental action to counteract the effects of the genetic disorder. Realization of one's errors is the beginning of wisdom, and true knowledge and effective action cannot be based on hypothetical, unproven and probably erroneous notions of what causal agencies might be involved.

All this, of course, is a long way from the political arena, from Negro militancy, Black Panthers, the Chicago trial, Bobby Seale, Malcolm X, and the Fanon myth. Yet there is a connection. Richard Crossman has pointed out that "Black Power has emerged as a revolutionary force not as a result of a refusal to make concessions in the sphere of civil rights but owing to the discovery that, even when civil rights are conceded in legislation and supported by judicial decision so that integration can theoretically take place, in fact it does not take place. Instead most of the black population remains an underprivileged proletariat. By making use of their newly acquired civil rights a small upper segment of the blacks can share the pursuit of happiness with their white fellow citizens. But they do so only by escaping from the ghettoes into which a lumpenproletariat is penned."

The deduction made from these facts by many activists is that it is prejudice, color bias, and intolerance which are responsible, and that only armed insurrection can succeed where more peaceful methods have failed. Such an analysis may fail for the same reason as compensatory education has failed. One important reason for the existence (and composition) of the "lumpenproletariat" Crossman speaks about may be the genetically determined low intelligence of many of those who have descended into it. (There are of course many other reasons which it would be foolish to disregard—physical illness, mental pathology, psychopathic and other personality traits not easily tolerated in our society, simple bad luck, and of course in some cases color prejudice as well. However, here we are concerned particularly with IQ, and the evidence certainly suggests that this is a very real and powerful factor.)*

But of course most of the people making up this "lumpenproletariat" are white. Again we are not dealing with a problem which is exclusively one of color, but rather of social class. Color comes into it, of course, but possibly mainly through the link between class and IQ, on the one hand, and race and IQ, on the other. If this is so, then clearly there is no partial solution to the problem (*i.e.* no solution

---

*There is good evidence that mental illness, criminality, and personality generally have strong roots in genetic constitution as well. I have summarized this in my book on *The Biological Basis of Personality*. Unfortunately little has been done to study the connection between these topics and race. It may be surmised, but cannot at the moment be supported by empirical research, that possibly here too genetically determined differences may be found. These differences may be favorable rather than unfavorable to the Negro; too little is known at the moment to make any kind of prediction. Here certainly seems to be an area of research which has been too long neglected, and which would repay study.

exclusively concerned with colored people). A solution is only possible in terms of a general abolition of the "lumpenproletariat" as a whole—both black and white. How such an ambitious undertaking can be realized is a problem well outside the psychologist's domain. It is not outside his domain, however, to point out the possibility that our present thinking about the color problem, social class, and racial prejudice may be over-simplified in the extreme. I would suggest that we do not even begin to know the precise nature of the problem, or the questions which we ought to be asking—let alone feel certain about the solutions which ought to be adopted.

CERTAINTY in all these matters is reserved for politicians. As a scientist I can only draw attention to certain possibilities, recount the facts which support (as well as those which speak against) these provisional hypotheses, and urge that those seriously concerned with the problems discussed should discard preconceived notions and take into account the results of painstaking research done during the past fifty years or so. Above all, it seems to me that the furtherance of more and better research into these complex questions is an urgent duty. In the U.S.A. such research at the moment may be vital, but even in Britain similar problems are building up threateningly, and it would be well if we were armed with knowledge when political decisions come to be made.

Can psychology really make a meaningful contribution? Let us look at the present situation. There are roughly speaking two main positions which people adopt when faced with the problem of color. On the one hand there is the reactionary, racist position which relies on suppression of all Negro aspirations, exemplified best in the South African policy of apartheid. On the other hand there is the policy of egalitarian enlightenment which believes in the (innate) equality of all human beings and pursues a policy of compensatory education and of equal opportunity for blacks.

It is not necessary to discuss the repressive policy. It stands condemned on ethical, humanistic and religious grounds, even if its outcome were not so clearly the threat of genocide or armed conflict. But the policy of enlightenment also may be faulted; not for its aims, but for its underlying beliefs which run counter to present-day knowledge. It raises hopes which may be impossible to fulfil; and disappointment may produce (and has already produced) a feeling among Negroes that all whites are the enemy, and that liberals are but false friends. A realistic policy needs not only compassion, but also knowledge; it is in the marriage of these two that our best hope for a genuine solution must lie.

Is such a solution possible? No one can know at the present time, but clearly our best efforts must be exerted towards such an end. Racial hatred is deadly; it can be fanned just as much by raising and then dashing justified hopes as by outright repression. Social scientists have not only the right but the duty to raise and freely discuss these problems, without worrying too much about being called "racists" by bigots on the one side, or "nigger-lovers" by bigots on the other. The situation is too grave for name-calling; it requires serious discussion, and above all research of a quality and on a scale which has hitherto been sadly missing. Even those who disagree with my tentative conclusions will be able to agree with me in this: only by proper research will the thesis of (partial) genetic determination of low Negro IQ be defeated. Until then, those concerned with public policy as well as those more interested in academic questions had better consider the genetic hypothesis as an alternative to the exclusively environmental hypothesis which has dominated our thoughts for far too long, and which has failed time and time again to produce the results, both political and research, which alone can support it.

THIS CONCLUSION is clearly opposed to that advocated by some U.S. scientific circles and by the British Society for

THE ISSUE

Teacher's Terminology: "Discipline" = Sociological Translation: "Securing conformity to role expectation norms"

1. Socialization to Differential Role Expectation Norms
2. Differentials in the Extent of Internalization of Norms and Controls
3. Differentials in Response to the System of Sanctions

DILEMMA OF COUNTERVAILING VALUES

"Even-handed Justice"	"Respect for Individual Difference"
Role Expectations and Behavioral Standards should be the same for every child	Educators must take Individual Differences into account. We cannot expect children from disadvantaged homes to behave like more advantaged children
Strategy: Maintain Traditional Norms and System of Sanctions	*Strategy:* Develop a dual set of Norms and Sanctions appropriate for the individual child

DILEMMA OF ACTION

1. Relatively weak position of Teacher in effecting primary types of Socialization	1. Normative disintegration of the Social System
2. Multiplication of Formal Rules vs. Level of Internalization of Norms	2. Dual Normative System with those to whom the 'Secondary' Norms apply being defined as 'Deviant'
3. Differential response to Traditional Sanctions which are primarily symbolic	
OUTCOME: Conformity vs. Alienation	OUTCOME: System Disintegration and/or Alienation

The Social Responsibility of Science

Social Responsibility in Science. Their view seems to be that it would be more "responsible" to sweep such unfashionable and ineluctable truths under the carpet. When racialism is such an explosive issue, they seem to be saying, it is irresponsible to bring to public notice facts which might be used to inflame protagonists even further. I am of course all in favor of scientists assuming social responsibility to the greatest degree possible; however, the terms used are not precisely enough defined to make discussion at all easy. As John Wren-Lewis pointed out, "what the demand for social responsibility always means, in practice, is simply the wish for scientific inquiry and application to be subservient to certain social values you happen to approve of." To which I may perhaps add ". . . and to certain procedural methods which you happen to favor." I agree with the social values of many of the scientists in Britain and America who so vehemently disagreed with Jensen (and indeed so does he, of course). Where we part company is in deciding upon the best method for achieving these common aims. I consider it an abrogation of the responsibilities of scientists to fail to communicate their discoveries and theories to the public. To do so is a responsibility which rests upon them by virtue of their status as scientists, and which is additional to any responsibilities they may have simply as members of society. The scientist owes the world objectivity, critical thought, and proof within the field of his own expertise. The world may or may not pay attention to what he has to say, but that is beyond his capacity to enforce. Ideological passion may reject the facts. But this does not exonerate him from the duty to make these facts known.

However opportune suppression of the truth may appear at any given moment, the evil consequences of such suppression are almost certainly much greater than any putative benefit which might be gained on a short-term basis. Habits of telling or of hiding the truth are quickly acquired, and may be difficult to change. Indoctrinate our social scientists with the notion that they should remain quiet when the truth seems to be such that it might be twisted by evil-intentioned persons to serve their own ends, and you are taking the first step in the direction of turning them from scientists into politicians.

Scientists share the belief, possibly naive, that "the truth shall make you free." Take this belief away from them and their whole motivation and reason for being is gone. The problems of race are truly terrifying but they can be overcome—not on the basis of suppressing unwelcome facts but by learning the truth and adjusting methods to facts. Problems are never solved by disregarding the evidence; they only get worse. What is needed, rather, is further evidence, more facts, greater knowledge. Only in this way will we be able to cope with our recurrent social problems.

THIS TYPE OF OBSERVATION is difficult to accept if you believe, as many people do, that such political steps as the enforcement of "desegregation" are adequate by themselves to solve the problem. Unfortunately hopes thus raised are easily dashed to the ground when "desegregation" is in fact put into operation; while a necessary and desirable first step, it clearly produces problems as well as solving others.

These problems are well delineated in the description by Jane Mercer of the events following desegregation of Riverside, California, schools. As her graphic account shows, teachers are faced with a whole series of dilemmas which defy solution. Usually, two alternative courses of action are fairly clearly defined, each of which has advantages and compensatory disadvantages. Any choice has genuine elements of tragedy in it, in the sense that it is not a "right" choice confronting a "wrong" one, but rather there are two highly regarded values between which a choice has to be made—there seems to be no way of retaining both.

Consider Mercer's first "dilemma," which is concerned with discipline. Table 4 shows the arguments and problems

THE ISSUE

Teacher's Terminology: 'Ability Grouping' = Sociological Translation: Control of Deviant
        Performance through Status Segregation

    1 Differentials in Academic Achievement
    2 Differentials in Performance on Measures of Ability
       (WISC, Peabody Picture Vocabulary, Raven's
       Progressive Matrices)

DILEMMA OF COUNTERVAILING VALUES

'Equality of Opportunity and Structural Integration'	'Concern for Individual Differences'
Children should be given equal access to knowledge and there should be structural integration of minority children into the elementary school	Each child should be grouped with those similar to his own grade level performance so that instruction can be geared to his ability and performance level
Strategy: Heterogeneous Grouping and Concern for Ethnic Balance in the Classroom	*Strategy:* Homogenous Grouping by Ability and/or Achievement Levels

DILEMMA OF ACTION

1 One teacher handling wide disparities in academic performance	1 Ceilings on expectations set in Motion a self-fulfilling prophecy
2 Reinforcing ethnic stereotypes	2 Evaluation by a 'Deviant normative structure' may produce unrealistic perceptions of societal norms
	3 Grouping is most stringent of the sanctions: defines the person out of his 'normal' role in the system into the role of an 'outsider'
OUTCOME: Enhanced Striving and Conformity vs. Alienation	OUTCOME: Structural Resegregation

The IQ Argument

150

involved. The colored and the white children now brought into contact in the same school room have been socialized in different ways, have "internalized" different standards and norms of behavior and respond differently to the usual sanctions of the school room. (To send a white child out of the room is regarded by that child as a punishment, to be avoided; Negro children may regard it as a reward and privilege!) The "dilemma of countervailing values" is clearly set out in the Table. If all children are treated alike (the ideal of "even-handed justice") then the teacher can produce conformity in some but at the risk of producing alienation in many other black children. If black children are treated differently, perhaps more leniently (the ideal of "respect for individual differences") then we face the disintegration of the whole system of discipline, possibly accompanied by alienation, this time on the part of the white children.

Table 5 shows another dilemma, namely that of "ability grouping" or streaming. Again we have a "dilemma of countervailing values." Should we treat all children as if they were equal, when in fact they clearly are not ("equality of opportunity"), or should we group children of equal ability together, so that each group can progress at its own rate ("concern for individual differences")? The first type of procedure produces enhanced striving and conformity in some, alienation in others, according to their ability. The second type of procedure in effect produces "structural re-segregation" in the sense that the less able groups will tend to be made up of black children, the more able groups of white children. Mercer quotes a touching account of how this dilemma presents itself in practice. This is a Negro teacher speaking:

"I had set up my classroom so that I could give more help to the children who needed it. And, as I was looking over my record, I wasn't thinking of color or anything else. I said, 'if I rearrange my room this way, I can give three or four or five more minutes to this child because I'll be able to reach them quicker than walking way over here where I had them all scattered about.' And when I arranged the room, I looked, and all the minority children, the Negroes, were clustered together. And so I said, 'Oh, I can't do this! I can't let this stay like this because any Negro parent coming in would say, Well, she's prejudiced too. Look what she's done to my child, she has all the Negroes clustered together.' She would not know the motive for my clustering. So I had to rearrange the class so that I had one colored child here and one white over here and so forth. I mean this really exists. . . ."

In America these types of problems tend to emerge in a racial form but that is of course not an essential feature of the underlying dilemma. Even if there were no Negroes or other minority groups in a country, there would still be bright and dull children, and the problems posed by their existence would be equally great, although the emotion invested would perhaps be less. As Jane Mercer says, "Dilemmas of countervailing values are perennial. A changing society is demanding that the public schools produce not only the form but the substance of equal educational opportunity for children of all socio-economic levels and all ethnic heritages. As school districts move beyond desegregation toward intergration, they will find that traditional solutions frequently create more problems then they solve and that rigid adherence to customary procedures may, in the end, defeat the avowed purposes of desegregation. There are no easy solutions to these fundamental dilemmas. Certainly a first step is to recognize that the dilemmas exist and that they are fundamentally value conflicts and must be handled as such. Regardless of which of the traditional values are pursued, we can anticipate outcomes which will militate against the goal of an integrated society."

THE SITUATION, THEN, is not one for easy "political" solutions. Anyone advocating such obvious panances as those set out in Tables 4 and 5, while ignoring the alternatives and the many undesirable consequences which flow from such measures, is simply playing with fire. Nor, as we have seen, does "compensatory education" in its traditional form have much to contribute. Inherited differences in ability are not eradicated by a few months of extra schooling. Desegregation, in the particular form which it has taken in the U.S.A., has clearly not been an unqualified success. Negroes themselves, particularly in the colleges, are forming "segregated" groups which refuse to have anything to do with white students; and similar phenomena are being observed in the schools. These troubles and difficulties may have been unavoidable, but I firmly believe that they have been exacerbated by the age-old habits of "conservatives" and "liberals" alike of acting on the basis, not of factual information, experiment, and properly validated scientific theory, but rather on the basis of intuition, subjective emotions and unrealistic theories of "human nature."

To pretend to know the answer to this general dilemma would be foolish; only doctrinaires rush in where knowledge is missing. But social scientists at least know the questions, and they also have the tools for conducting the research which alone will show us the best way of dealing with the educational, racial, and moral problems raised. Do we have the wisdom to seek for these answers, patiently and with scientific impartiality, or will we continue to attempt to solve human problems by reference to outdated political prejudices? The answer to this question might be more important than we think. It may determine whether our children shall live or die.

BRIEF BIBLIOGRAPHY

L. E. Andor, "Aptitudes and Abilities of the Black Man in Sub-Saharan Africa," National Institute of Personnel Research, South African Council for Scientific and Industrial Research (1966).

N. Bayley, "Comparisons of Mental and Motor Test Scores for Ages 1-15 Months by Sex, Birth Order, Race, Geographical Location, and Education of Parents," *Journal of Child Development*, No. 36 (1965).

J. S. Coleman et. al., *Equality of Educational Opportunity*, U.S. Dept. of Health, Education and Welfare (1966).

M. Deutsch, I. Katz and A. R. Jensen (eds.), *Social Class, Race and Psychological Development*, (Holt, Rinehart & Winston, 1968).

T. Dobzhansky, *Mankind Evolving: the Evolution of the Human Species*, (Yale University Press, 1962).

H. J. Eysenck, *The Biological Basis of Personality*, (C. C. Thomas, 1970).

G. A. Harrison and J. Peel (eds.), "Biosocial Aspects of Race," *Journal of Biosocial Science* (Supp. 1, 1969).

J. McV. Hunt, *Intelligence and Experience*, (Ronald Press, 1961).

A. R. Jensen, "Estimation of the Limits of Heritability of Traits by Comparison of Monzygotic and Dizygotic Twins," *Proceedings of the National Academy of Science of the United States of America*, No. 58 (1967).

A. R. Jensen et. al., "Environment, Heredity and Intelligence," Harvard Reprint Series, No. 2 (1969).

J. L. Jink and D. W. Fulker, "Comparisons of the Biometrical Genetical MAVA, and Classical Approaches to the Analysis of Human Behavior," *Psychological Bulletin*, No. 73 (1970).

R. E. Kuttner (ed.), *Race and Modern Science: a Collection of Essays by Biologists, Anthropologists, Sociologists and Psychologists*, (Social Science Press, 1967).

M. M. de Lemos, "The Development of Conservation in Aboriginal Children," *International Journal of Psychology*, No. 4 (1969).

G. S. Lesser, G. Fifer and D. H. Clark, "Mental Abilities of Children from Different Social-Class and Cultural Groups," *Monographs of the Society for Research in Child Development*, No. 30 (1965).

J. Macnamara, *Bilingualism and Primary Education*, (Edinburgh University Press, 1966).

M. Manosevitz, G. Lindzey and D. D. Thiessen (eds.), *Behavioral Genetics: Method and Research*, (Appleton-Century-Crofts, 1969).

W. A. Martin, "Word Fluency: a Comparative Study," *Journal of Genetic Psychology*, No. 114 (1969).

C. E. Noble, "Race, Reality and Experimental Psychology," *Perspectives in Biology and Medicine*, No. 13 (1969).

A. M. Shuey, *The Testing of Negro Intelligence*, (Social Science Press, 1966).

J. N. Spuhler (ed.), *Genetic Diversity and Human Behavior*, (Aldine Publishing Co., 1967).

S. G. Vandenberg (ed.), *Progress in Human Behavior Genetics: Recent Reports on Genetic Syndromes, Twin Studies, and Statistical Advances*, (Johns Hopkins Press, 1968).

P. E. Vernon, *Intelligence and Cultural Environment*, (Methuen, 1969).

Western Regional Conference on Testing Problems: Proceedings 1968 (for study by Jane Mercer), Educational Testing Service, Princeton.

ABOUT THE AUTHOR

H. J. Eysenck enjoys a world-wide reputation as a scientist and author. He was born in Germany, educated in France and England, and has lectured at various American universities. He is at present Director of the Institute of Psychiatry at the Maudsley Hospital in London, and Professor of Psychology at the University there. He is editor-in-chief of an international scientific journal, *Behaviour Research and Therapy*, and has contributed more than 300 articles to various scientific journals. Among his thirty published books are several famous Penguin titles which have sold in the millions of copies (*Uses and Abuses of Psychology, Sense and Nonsense in Psychology*, and *Know Your Own I.Q.*) as well as *Anxiety and Hysteria* (1957), *Experiments with Drugs* (1963), *Crime and Personality* (1964), and *The Biological Basis of Personality* (1968).